WHEN THE BAD TIMES ARE OVER FOR GOOD

WHEN THE BAD TIMES ARE OVER FOR GOOD

Transforming Trouble Into Triumph

GERALD MANN

McCracken Press

New York

McCracken Press™

An imprint of Multi Media Communicators, Inc.

575 Madison Avenue, Suite 1006

New York, NY 10022

Cover Design, Vin Mastellone

Library of Congress Catalog Card Number: 93-078997

ISBN 1-56977-560-5

10 9 8 7 6 5 4 3 2 1

Printed in the United States of America

This book is for
the people of Riverbend
without whom...

Contents

Acknowledgments

God has always sent people to hold onto me as I stood on the precipice of suffering. They have made this book possible. How to name them? How to name their blessings great and small?

You just have to start and hope those you leave out loved you without the thought of being acknowledged, and love you still.

Riverbend. A rare people. You somehow learned that the only thing radical about "Christian" behavior is the way we love. You not only gave me the time to write this, you "let me go" and "let me be" long before that.

Anita Tyler. Typing the manuscript was the least of your gifts to me. Is it ten years since I went with you to make arrangements for your Katy's funeral? And three years since you finally climbed out of the pit and said yes to life again? I don't remember. But I do remember your stubborn insistence that your grieving would have been shortened if I had written this sooner. Without that affirmation I couldn't have continued.

Francis (Doc) and Joyce Heatherly. No strangers to the re-assembly of broken pieces yourselves. You believed in me and were so kind to me when I ventured to let you see this first.

Fred Smith, Jr. You and Bob Buford gave me a second life in the pastorate and the nerve to write again.

Wally and Rosie Lundgren. Thanks for the sanctuary by the sea where these words took form. Who but God could have planned for our paths to cross at a time when we were both trying to grope through our grief?

Lois. The saint. You have written a masterpiece with your life while I have scratched pitifully with my pen.

And Cindy. You have never heard me say "I love you" with your ears. I pray to God you will hear me say it on these pages.

Introduction

There are only two instances in which the bad times will be over for good. One is supposedly when we die. In the meantime, we are told that our task is to cope and hope, to hang on and make the best of it. We are to grin and bear it till we reach the other side. Well, the power to cope is an admirable quality, and sometimes all we can do is put one foot in front of the other. But coping isn't living as we were meant to live.

This book is about the second way the bad times are over for good, when we go beyond *coping* to *conquering*. Trouble doesn't have to be merely endured; it can be transformed.

For example, I'm thinking of Richard of Bethel.[1] In the 1800s, a group of German humanitarians were moved to do something about the squalid conditions of the many physically handicapped people who were warehoused and discarded in attics and trash heaps around the country. They built Bethel, which means "house of God" in Hebrew. Bethel became a model of care and nurture for the helpless.

Dr. Leo Bustad, a professor of veterinary medicine, visited there several years ago. At one point his host asked him if he would mind visiting Richard, a spastic who talked in guttural bursts that had to be translated by his nurse. Usually Richard did not receive guests because he was extremely sensitive to his condition and did not want to make strangers uneasy.

However, he had a profound interest in animals and wanted to meet someone like Dr. Bustad who treated their suffering. Bustad found a sensitive, bright, and beautiful soul trapped inside a pitifully crippled body.

Through the translator, Richard asked questions which revealed that he had acquired considerable knowledge about animals. As Bustad started to leave, Richard asked if there were any Indians in the professor's classes in America. The professor answered yes, not knowing if Richard was referring to native Americans or natives of India.

Later, the host told Bustad that Richard had meant natives of India. "You see, Richard supports an orphan in India," said his host. "Besides his eye muscles, Richard has control of only two toes on his right foot. With the use of mirrors and years of exercise, he has learned to paint. He sells the paintings and uses the proceeds to raise the child."

Richard of Bethel is a shining example of making the bad times over for the sake of a higher good, of using evil and suffering as a tool for transforming trouble into triumph.

FANTASIZE OR METABOLIZE

Much of the Eastern and the Western world try to fantasize away the reality of pain and tragedy. Eastern mysticism says suffering is an illusion that comes from our attempt to be individuals apart from the "world soul." Therefore, cease to be, and you'll cease to hurt. In Western culture we fantasize suffering by taking the attitude, "it won't happen to me," or, "if it does, they will find a pill or a program to cure it."

The Christian approach to suffering keeps getting lost in our frantic attempts to avoid pain. What is the "Christian approach"? To *metabolize* suffering—to accept it, embrace it, ingest it, digest it, and transform it into strength. That's what Richard of Bethel did. He didn't try to fantasize away tragedy; he metabolized it.

Jesus of Nazareth also endured suffering. He didn't run nor did He fantasize. He didn't merely hang on until He reached "the other side of the river." He ingested, digested, and transformed the Cross into the Resurrection.

Yet most of us are unprepared for and ill-equipped to face the bad times. We keep looking for magic medicine and medicine men—dispensers of herbs, elixirs, new diets, tummy tucks— and miracles in the name of God, too.

Life magazine interviewed Lee Atwater shortly before he died of brain cancer.[2] His life typifies the approach to suffering which most of us take. Atwater was the young political phenomenon who planned and executed George Bush's landslide presidential victory in 1988. He grew up with two burning ambitions: to manage a successful presidential campaign and to chair the National Republican Party before he reached the age of thirty-five.

> **"What is the 'truly Christian approach'?**
> **To metabolize suffering—to accept it,**
> **embrace it, ingest it, digest it, and trans-**
> **form it into strength."**

He was, by his own account, ruthless and relentless. He carried three books with him at all times: Plato's *Republic*, Machiavelli's *The Prince*, and Tzun Tsu's *The Art of War*. His strategy was cruelly simplistic: First, find the enemy's weakness and attack without mercy or pause. Second, find a way to make the enemy look small and comical both in his own eyes and in the eyes of his potential supporters.

Do you remember Bush's opponent in 1988? Michael Dukakis. Do you remember how Atwater used the Willie Horton case (Horton was a paroled offender who offended again) to convince the world that Dukakis was soft on crime? Do you remember "little Dukakis" riding in a tank with that *funny* helmet on his head which made him look like "a squirrel," as Atwater put it?

At age thirty-four Lee Atwater had accomplished both of his goals. Then the brain tumor was discovered. He took his usual approach—the approach most of us would take.

First he called his team together and doled out assignments. They were to learn about the type of cancer, find its weaknesses, and attack. After examining the alternatives, Atwater chose the most radical treatment—radioactive pellets funneled straight into the brain. The treatment was unsuccessful. Next came a worldwide search for more exotic cures: herbs, sweat lodges, Indian Shamans, diets, sugar shocks, astrologists. These didn't work either. Then came prayer and preachers. (They all get down to these eventually.) Hands-layer-ons, slayers in the Spirit, liberals, fundamentalists, tongue-speakers, non-speakers. Atwater tried them all.

Atwater was fantasizing his tragedy. But that's not the end of the story. His last article was a haunting cry to all of us who face suffering.

> Long before I was struck with cancer, I felt something stirring in American society. It was a sense among the people that something was missing from their lives. Something crucial. I was trying to position the Republican Party to take advantage of it, but I wasn't sure what "it" was. My illness has helped me to see that what was missing in society is what was missing in me: a little heart and a lot of Brotherhood.
>
> The '80's were about acquiring—acquiring wealth, power and prestige. I know about those. I acquired more than most. But you can acquire all you want and still feel empty. What power I wouldn't give for a little more time with my family...with my friends.
>
> It took a deadly illness to put me eye to eye with the truth. But it's a truth that this country—caught up

in its ruthless ambitions and moral decay—can learn on my dime. I don't know who will lead us through the '90's but they must be made to speak to this spiritual vacuum at the heart of American society—this tumor of the soul.[3]

These are the words of a true son of Western materialism. No one prepared him to metabolize the bad times for good. Yet in his parting words, we can hear him saying that his suffering has no point unless he can *use it* to point to a higher good.

One time I read where Dostoevsky said that throughout his life on earth he prayed only to be worthy of his suffering. I thought, *Well, there's the Russians for you. They've always been a melancholy bunch. Wouldn't we all be if we were raised in a country that went from one barbarism to another?* Now I know what he meant. He understood that if we are going to live in the real world, we must find a way to use our pain rather than deny it or avoid it.

How do I know this? What qualifies me to write a book about turning trouble into triumph?

MY TROUBLE TO TRANSFORM

I married my high school sweetheart when I was twenty, and she was eighteen. Eleven months later our first daughter was born. During those months I also became a believer and began studying for the ministry.

Before we even knew Lois was pregnant, she had German measles—rubella, or "three-day measles" as it was known then. We didn't even know enough to worry. During the seventh month of pregnancy, someone mentioned there could be potential damage to the fetus. I immediately phoned the doctor, a country general practitioner. When I sounded alarmed, he scolded me. "Now, Jerry," he chided, "if your child has only four toes, or four fingers, or one foot; will you love it any less?"

"Oh, if that's all we're talking about," I said, "why, heck no!" But that wasn't *all* we were talking about. Our daughter was thirteen months old before we got "real" enough to start trying to find out what was wrong.

First a pediatrician said she was just hyperactive and a little behind in learning to talk. Then a neurologist checked her out and watched her play around in the office for about ten minutes. He took me into his office and shut the door. "She's severely retarded, son. My advice is to put her in an institution somewhere, take that pretty little wife of yours home, and get her pregnant again. Maybe your second one will come out okay."

I was a rich kid, a football star attending college on scholarship, and a newly converted believer. This just couldn't be!

I had given my life to follow in Jesus' steps and forego the wealth, power, and prestige awaiting me in the family's business. And my child, my only child, had been assaulted in the warmth of her mother's womb by an insidious, mindless virus which would alter our lives forever.

I had read the New Testament. Jesus healed, and He promised that we could, too, if we believed. And I believed. I placed my hands on little Cindy many a night, praying for her healing. When nothing happened, I was certain the fault had to lie with me. It certainly didn't lie with the child. Nor could it lie with God, for He was good and loving and delivered His people.

So I tried harder. And harder. Some months later, we learned Cindy was not retarded. "Just deaf." When the audiologist tried to break the news to us gently, he was visibly confused to find us overjoyed to learn that she was "just deaf."

"Just deaf"—little did we know. Deafness and hearing

impairment (did you know there was a difference?) are arguably the most misunderstood handicaps in our society. When Helen Keller, who was both deaf and blind, was asked which malady she would select if given the choice, she said blindness over deafness without hesitation.

We immediately took the Lee Atwater approach: Learn the enemy and attack. The "experts" told us that new and great strides were being made with the deaf. Our daughter should go to a speech and hearing school which prohibited the use of sign language. With proper training, she could lead a normal life within a hearing society.

She and Lois started to school together in Houston. I pastored a small church there and commuted to seminary three hundred miles away for seven years through two degrees. Lois taught Cindy every word she ever knew. They worked day and night. All conversation was speech therapy. I took my doctorate in philosophy of religion, for that was the discipline where we addressed the question of how to account for a God who is both good and all-powerful and yet allowed the existence of rubella babies.

When Cindy was eight years old, she belonged nowhere. She was out of place in the hearing world, and she was out of place among deaf people who "spoke" sign language. Sign language is a language of its own, not simply a method of speaking English with one's hands.

There was only one place that held promise for a deaf child who could "eventually make it" in a hearing world, as the experts kept telling us. There was a school in Northampton, Massachusetts, two thousand miles away. The annual tuition was exactly the size of my salary now that I was *Doctor* Mann and pastoring a county seat church.

We managed financially; we died emotionally. The day we deposited little Cindy at the dorm, she held on for dear life. "If you love me, Daddy," she said in her slow over-pronouncing way, using every word Lois had taught her with precision, "you will not leave me here." Her first letter came, and I still have it: "Every dark I look at moon. I say, 'Daddy look at moon like me.' That way we together when it dark. When moon not at home I look at star. So I not know if we together. I cry. Can you see star, Daddy?"

When she was home for the summers and holidays, we got a foretaste of things to come. By then, Stacey, our second daughter who was bright, verbal, and sociable had become the painful reminder to Cindy of what might have been. The spontaneous outbursts of rage began. Cindy would become violent as though possessed. We couldn't leave her at home alone with Stacey and our young son.

At sixteen, Cindy came home for good. That was sixteen years ago. I have always thought that having to deal with the death of a child is the worst of all grief experiences. I cannot imagine how people get through it. However, having to deal with the life of a child whose pain and suffering will outlive you is also unimaginable if you haven't experienced it. It's a living hell that goes on without boundaries.

Not belonging in the world of the deaf or the world of the hearing, Cindy gravitated to hearing people who would use her. Her first boyfriend was hearing impaired. He had enough hearing to use the telephone and communicate quite well with hearing people. He also introduced Cindy to drugs. The next twelve years was a treadmill of drugs, thugs, rehab centers, halfway houses, and four different colleges.

Finally sober, Cindy married a hearing boy at age twenty-five. Our first grandchild was born. Then they separated when the baby was three years old, after four years of violent eruptions.

Before long Cindy began to associate with those who made it apparent that our granddaughter's well-being was endangered. Then suddenly her estranged husband, deeply in debt and unemployed, fled with the child. The cavalry—Lois and I— came to the rescue, found the baby, and brought her home. Divorce papers were filed. Cindy agreed to let us raise the baby if we joined her in the custody battle with her husband.

Just before I began this book, the story took a strange turn. Our daughter hired a lawyer and joined her estranged husband in contesting us for custody of the granddaughter who has been living with us for over a year. Now this little girl is going to live with her father. We have packed up a beautiful little girl, now four years old, and told her good-bye, after bonding with her, of course.

I've been waiting thirty-two years to tell the story of our struggle because I wanted to be able to share how wonderfully it all turned out. I wanted to announce that after years of sorrow and woe the sun came shining through the clouds, and we all lived happily ever after.

Now I have come to realize that the sun has been shining all along. Throughout this long nightmare, we've been transforming our trouble into triumph. Remarkable things have happened, in spite of the bad times.

For one thing I've been gleefully in love with the same woman for thirty-three years. Of the twenty-three couples who had children in that first speech and hearing class, only Lois and I are still together. During the years when Lois had so little of herself to give to anyone except Cindy, I was commuting to school. When she had nothing to give, I wasn't asking. We learned the art of building a relationship on small bits of quality time. We never had the luxury of getting bored with each other. We've loved and laughed from the Motel 6 to the Nile Hilton to the African bush.

Another remarkable thing: Our two younger children are great kids by any measurement. They have not been negatively marked by the trauma of Cindy's trouble.

And there's the blessing of our great church that started with sixty souls, who have reached another four thousand by now. We focus on the four B's: the bruised, the battered, the broken, and the bored. Our church is what Kennon Callahan calls a M.A.S.H. tent on the frontier of a hurting world.[4] We're always out of resources. There are more patients than we can treat. But there's pure excitement all the time. The garbage can is our symbol and "We Recycle," our motto. You can come to Riverbend and dump your garbage—your sins and hurts and regrets. And here you can begin again.

You see, I understand these people. I was born to be with them. I have come to believe that God never uses anyone strategically until He's allowed them to hurt deeply. *Strategically* means for a particular, made-to-order purpose. God strategically placed me where I could help the hurting because I've been there.

In my study of philosophy, I never found an answer to the age-old problem of evil and suffering that would hold rational water. But in looking for one I was exposed to the thoughts of the great minds of the centuries. More importantly, I'm not afraid that any human mind can destroy the reality of God.

On the pages that follow, I will be sharing ideas, exercises, and techniques I have discovered for transforming trouble into triumph. There's very little that is original. To be original is not to say what's never been said, but to say exactly what you believe because you've found it to be true in your own trek through life (which is not an original statement, but I can't remember where I got it).

But before we move on, I must share another remarkable thing: I have no animosity or rancor toward God or Cindy. I have had plenty toward both in times past. (Have you ever been so mad at God that you wanted Him to kill you and then became angrier when He wouldn't?)

Clearly, we made great mistakes in parenting Cindy. We were teenagers when she was born. We were barely out of our twenties when she reached puberty. If there is blame to be passed around, I deserve the lion's share. I was often an absentee father. Also, the final chapters of Cindy's life are unwritten. She possesses an amazing toughness of character. And God is not easily defeated when it comes to His little ones.

I see Cindy as my "pebble in the heart." Do you know what that is? The human heart is a muscle that is nourished by arteries. The heart also has hidden dormant channels that are sometimes activated when one of the arteries gets clogged. If the blockage is not too sudden and the heart has time, it builds collateral channels around the blockage. This blockage never goes away. The heart must bypass it and keep on pumping.

I call these naturally bypassed occlusions "pebbles in the heart." I know about such things because I literally have a "pebble" in my heart as I write this. At the age of forty-two I had coronary bypass surgery. The graft that bypassed the blockage has now worn out, but my heart is strong. In the eleven years since the surgery, my heart has built collaterals around the pebble, and it no longer threatens my life.

In the same way, suffering no longer threatens my spiritual life. Cindy's problem is and probably always will be "in my heart"—a blockage, an obstruction to my faith. I have released her and her little girl to the graces of God.

Amazingly, the result has been positive. Our granddaughter spends many happy days with us. Cindy is plowing her own furrows for the first time. We have a pleasant relationship with our former son-in-law. In days to come, we shall hold them all as "pebbles," but we shall build collaterals and keep on pumping.

1

Grace Is the Grit

Birds have gizzards. Gizzards are for grit. The birds eat the grit, which allows them to grind, digest, and metabolize their food—God's grace is the grit that allows us to transform trouble into triumph. Yet most people don't know what grace is. And many who do understand it haven't transferred it from the head level to the gizzard level, where it counts.

Grace can be understood and not felt. I understood it long before I internalized it. I wrote papers on the subject; I preached on grace and thrilled listeners. I was well-nigh an expert on grace before it became grace *for me*.

But Lois, who cares little for theological definitions, had grace. She felt it in her bones, and it has empowered her for years.

You can understand God's grace and not feel it, and you can feel it and not understand it. I want to help you do both.

UNDERSTANDING GOD'S GRACE—
A STORY

To complete my last semester for a master's degree, I needed a two-hour elective course. I searched the class schedule for a "laugher"—something on the order of "Tractor Driving on the Mission Field." But the only elective my schedule allowed was Advanced Greek. The professor, who had never given an A in the course, delighted in deflating the egos of the smart guys.

Six of us—all doctoral candidates—showed up the first day with fear and trembling. He called us to order and held up a little black book. "This is the grade book for the course," he said. He stared at us, one at a time.

"There has never been an A entered in this book. No one has ever deserved or earned it. But this year will be different.

"I have already written your names in the book. And I have already entered your grades. It makes no difference how much or how little you study. It makes no difference how high you score on tests. Your grade will not change. Everyone gets an A." His face hinted a smile, and then we got down to business.

I learned more Greek than I thought possible. By the end of the semester, most of us could sight-read any passage in the Greek New Testament.

> **POINT:** The taskmaster had taken away our fear of failure from the start. We got an A simply for enrolling and *that* gave us a power to perform, a freedom to surpass our usual limits.

God gives you an A simply for enrolling in His course. When you sign on to trust and follow Him in Christ, you've passed with honors. There is no final exam!

> **POINT:** God's grace means that our standing with Him does not depend on who we are and what we've done. It depends on who *He* is and what *He*'s done. He takes so much delight in us that He makes us valedictorians simply for signing up.

I can hear you saying: "Are you telling me that I can do as I please and still be okay with God?" Yep. "Does this mean I don't have to be good in order to be safe with God?" Yep. Your standing doesn't depend on you; it depends on Him.

However, there was a guy in the Greek class who didn't use the professor's grace as a power to perform, but rather as a license to loaf. He never came to class, and the next we saw him was at commencement.

"People want to know if God's going to keep them or throw them away."

But the professor kept his promise. The guy received an A. He didn't learn any Greek, and he had to live with the fact that he was a freeloader. But to this day, the A is still on his transcript.

God's grace is radical that way. His gifts to us are the same whether we use them as a power to perform or as a license to loaf. He's willing to take that chance.

I do a live, call-in television program called "Common Sense Religion" on Sunday evenings. People call from all over the country, and I never know what's coming.

Far and away the most frequently asked question is the question of eternal safety. People want to know if God's going to keep them or throw them away. They want to be sure they have kept the minimum requirements for divine acceptance. This tells me that in spite of the millions of dollars and hours spent by the church, people still don't understand that God is a grace-God. There's nothing you can ever do to make Him love you more than He already does. There's nothing you can ever do to make Him love you less either.

Grace and Face

Your face is the window of your soul. The Greeks recognized this long ago. In their plays, they cast the characters with masks which were called *persona*. Your face is your *persona*.

Will Rogers said you can always trust a man if dogs and kids follow him around. Why? Because dogs and kids are great face-readers!

Tom T. Hall, of country music fame, has a song that goes, "The story of your life is in your face. It's written there in little subtle lines." We speak of putting on our "game face" or "poker face." We describe people as being "stone-faced."

Karl Menninger describes the "negativistic personality" in his book, *The Vital Balance.* He says the telltale sign of this malady is in the face.[1] In the first chapter of John's gospel, he says in essence:

> We finally saw God's face. [The Word became a human being and, full of grace and truth, lived among us. We saw his glory. v. 14] And guess what! His face was full of grace! [Out of the fullness of his grace he has blessed us all, giving us one blessing after another. No one has ever seen God. The only Son, who is the same as God and is at the Father's side, he has made him known. vv. 16-18]

What happens to God's face when He thinks of you? Does He frown? Does He cry? Does He shake His head in disgust? No! God smiles with delight when He thinks of you!

Once Thomas Jefferson was traveling across country on horseback during his tenure as president. He and his entourage came to a river which they had to ford.

An old tattered beggar stood beside the stream like a hitch-hiker. As Jefferson's men forded the river one by one, the beggar looked at each and said nothing. When it came Jefferson's turn, the old man asked him for a lift. The president obliged, but when they reached the other side, the president's men began to scold the beggar.

"Why did you bother the president?" they chided. "You could've been shot!" "I didn't know he was the president," said the beggar. "All I know is that on some faces is written the word *no,* and on some faces is written the word *yes.* He had a yes face!"[2]

God has a yes face. We've had God all wrong for too long. He's out to *get us* all right. But not like a predator gets its prey. He's out to get us like a lover wins the object of his desire!

Grace and Space

What does God's grace mean for me personally? I've already mentioned eternal safety. Not only am I okay with God, I always will be, whether I use His fondness for me as a license to loaf or a power to perform. The only thing I have to do is enroll in Jesus Christ.

I have a space. I am not a bubble on the cosmic ocean that rises for a moment and is then reabsorbed, losing all identity. I have a space marked "Reserved." I'm somebody permanent.

> *"Not only am I okay with God, I always will be, whether I use His fondness for me as a license to loaf or a power to perform."*

A fellow philosophy major, gifted minister, and pilgrim in the faith chucked it all after a bad experience with his first parish. He became a brilliant attorney; he also became an alcoholic.

We hunted and fished together some. The last time I saw him, he asked, "Do you know anything in this entire world, visible or invisible, that is for certain?" "Only that God loves me," I said. He looked soulfully into the crackling campfire and mused, "Wish I could believe that." Some years later he took his life. He did not know he had a space.

I visited the catacombs beneath the ancient Roman Coliseum where the early Christians died. I was surprised to find that along with prominent symbols of the cross and the fish was the symbol of the anchor. When the storms of death blew, they had something which held them into the wind. For them grace meant space.

Grace and Place

Grace also means that I have a place, a recognized rank in the pecking order. And don't we all want that! That's what superstar mania is all about. People pay money just to touch somebody famous.

I was at a think tank not long ago, an invitation-only affair for senior pastors. At the get-acquainted party, I didn't talk to one pastor who failed to tell me how big his church was and ask me the size of mine. When we learned there was one guy who had thirteen thousand people per week, the meeting was spoiled. Every time a subject came up, we all waited to hear his opinion, which he was more than willing to give. We felt ours didn't matter.

As I mentioned earlier, I almost died at the age of forty-two with heart trouble. As we were rushing to surgery, I had to face the reality of my death for the first time—not death in general, but mine in particular.

I wasn't afraid; I was angry. There was so much I wanted to do. I was bitter and sad at the prospect of dying because I felt that my life hadn't *"mattered enough yet."* In a word, I hadn't achieved the place I thought I should achieve.

Facing death up close helped me see that God's grace insures me a place *already!*

David Redding, the gifted author of such books as *Jesus Makes Me Laugh,* said he received a long distance phone call.[3]

The voice said, "Dr. Redding, I've just finished listening to your book on tape, and I must tell you my story." Redding, like the rest of us who write, likes to listen to people who've read his books.

The caller's name was Vernon Coldiron. He said that five years earlier he had worked for a large company where he had been having problems with his boss. To complicate matters, he had also developed an addiction to Valium.

One morning he took his usual dosage. He remembers nothing after that except what he's been told. He arrived at the company offices armed with a gun and promptly took his boss hostage.

A S.W.A.T. team was summoned. After several hours of aborted atempts to talk him down, the authorities called in a sharpshooter. The rifle bullet entered under one eye and exited the opposite temple. Months later Coldiron awakened from deep coma and realized he was blind. He was obviously terrified, not knowing where he was. Then, he said, he heard the clear quiet voice of God from somewhere in the darkness. The voice said, "Vernon, I'm going to give you another chance."

Our God is the kind who comes and finds us in the darkness so that He can hand out more chances.

Coldiron went on to tell Redding that he now lived alone in a one room apartment, rejected by his family and friends and without any company save his tape recorder and radio.

Then he said, "But, Dr. Redding, I want you to know that what you say in your book is correct. God is with me. I can never be alone.[4] *Grace means having a place of importance which makes being important unimportant.*

Grace and Pace

God's grace, His unqualified delight in us, also affects the pace or cadence of our lives. We hear a lot about America's *decadence.* The word usually refers to sexual infidelity and irresponsibility. Our obsession with sex is only a symptom, a result of life being out of sync, i.e., de-cadent. The first thing a bored society does is rush to bed. It loses its steadiness of pace.

To know how God really feels about us takes the worry out of our hurry. H. M. Stanley, the British journalist and agnostic who went to Africa to find Dr. David Livingston, said of the great Christian missionary, "Whether he was walking, running, or dashing, he always moved with an unworried step."[5]

One of the greatest stories Jesus ever told was about a man who had two sons. One was a rebel who took his share of the family fortune and wasted it. When he came home, broke and broken, the father *ran* to meet him and threw a party.

The other son was a robot who obeyed all of the rules. He came in from the fields where he labored faithfully every day and discovered the party. He refused to go in, but the father *begged* him to come.

Neither boy had ever really known his father. One thought him a taskmaster to be eluded. The other thought him a taskmaster to be placated with hard work. They didn't know they'd already made A's in sonship, *simply by being in their father's house.*

Well, that's what grace is: A *face*—God's yes face. He smiles every time He thinks of you. This means you have a *space*, a permanent acceptance, and a *place*—a rank, an importance which makes being important unimportant, and a *pace*—you can hurry without worry.

So after understanding grace at the head level, what about the heart stuff? How do we transfer God's delight to the heart level?

FEELING GRACE: ANOTHER STORY

Transferring God's delight from my head to my heart didn't happen all at once, hasn't happened fully yet, and never will this side of heaven. Sometimes I forget God's grace or reject it or lose my faith in it and have to recapture it. It often grabs me in what I call "milestone moments."

The first milestone moment for me was when I knew God was there, that He'd always been there, and that He loved me. The second milestone moment was when God became personal to me in the person of Jesus of Nazareth who is called the Christ. What happens to your outlook and energy and lifestyle when grace becomes more than a concept, when you know it on the heart level?

For me, it changed everything—the way I looked at God, others, and myself. Most important, it changed the way I looked at my suffering. I have experienced firsthand that the underlying Reality of all that exists is gracious. God is personal and delightful and with me.

And this Gracious Ground, which is God's other name, has become the grit in my gizzard for grinding trouble into triumph. The chessboard of reality is not black with white squares—that is, evil with a little good sprinkled here and there. It is white with black squares—basically good with evil overlaid here and there.

How do I know that? From a few experiences and a lot of choices. Whenever the bottom has fallen out, I have found God at the bottom. Or rather, He has found me.

2

Trouble's the Trigger

It's no coincidence that when the psychotherapists began to use healthy people instead of sick people to study human nature, they also began to reconfirm the biblical view of human nature.

Psychotherapist Fritz Perls, the father of Gestalt therapy, once spoke at a conference that a friend of mine attended. At one point, someone asked him to describe his method of treating patients.

He said, "I imagine that the patient is standing on the bank of a raging river which he must cross in order to be whole. There are rocks sticking out of the river at intermittent points all the way to the opposite bank. But they are far enough apart so that the patient must leap from one to the other if he is to cross.

"My task is to help him find the courage to leap to one rock at a time."

Someone in the audience said, "But what if the patient falls in?" Perls supposedly looked at the questioner for a moment and replied, "It is better to fall in than to stand on the bank wishing."

Then Perls went on to say, "People who spend their lives trying to avoid trouble are never fully born." According to my friend, he then said something that has stuck with me: "Trouble can trigger disintegration or reintegration. If it triggers disintegration, the patient is really no worse off than he was to begin with."

Think of that: *To spend your life running away from trouble is as bad as being paralyzed by it!* To spend your life in a shell is as unwholesome as being overcome by life's hurts.

Bruce Larson visited and studied at several psychiatric treatment centers in preparation for his book, *The Meaning and Mystery of Being Human.* He says that although the centers held widely divergent views of human nature, they all agreed on two things: (1) that the inordinate desire for safety is a symptom of mental illness, and (2) that the ability to take risks and even to welcome them is a symptom of mental health.[1]

If grace is the grit which allows us to metabolize our pain, then trouble is the trigger for reintegration of life. *Reintegration* describes the process of putting life back together after it's fallen apart. The biblical words *Salvation,* and *to be saved* can also be translated "wholeness" and "to be made whole."

The book of James, a collection of practical instructions and guidelines for early Christians who were beset with all kinds of troubles, begins with an amazing statement: "Consider yourselves fortunate when all kinds of trials come your way" (James 1:2). Sounds masochistic, doesn't it? Who in his right mind would welcome trouble?

I suppose James knew that trouble was coming whether he welcomed it or not. At any rate, he doesn't leave us there. He goes on to outline several positive, wholesome things that trouble can trigger in our lives.

TOUGH FAITH

"When your faith succeeds in facing such trials," says James, "the result is the ability to endure" (James 1:3). Trouble can trigger tough faith. "Tough faith"—what is that? I can tell you what it's not. It's not unexamined faith. We tend to believe because we've been told or because we're afraid. Had I been born in Iraq, I would probably be a Muslim calling Christians infidels.

Tough faith is not fairweather faith, where we believe because it's comfortable to do so. Tough faith is when you keep believing without supportive evidence.

There's a wonderful story in the Bible which illustrates tough faith. Elijah, God's prophet, has announced to the king that a drought has come upon the land because of the king's wickedness (1 Kings 17). Immediately, Elijah hides in the wilderness by one of the last running brooks in the country. When the stream runs dry, God tells Elijah to go to a village named Zarephath; there a widow will feed him.

> *"We tend to believe because we've been told or because we're afraid. Had I been born in Iraq, I would probably be a Muslim calling Christians infidels.... Tough faith is when you keep believing without supportive evidence."*

When he arrives, he meets the widow on the outskirts of the village. She's down to her last handful of flour and a bit of olive oil and is gathering firewood for the last meal she and her small son will ever eat.

You can imagine her reaction when healthy, strapping Elijah shows up ordering food. "By the living LORD your God, I swear" (notice she says, *your* God, not *mine*) "that I don't have any bread. All I have is a handful of flour in a bowl and a bit of olive oil in a jar.... That will be our last meal, and then we will starve to death" (1 Kings 17: 12).

Elijah then says something that must have sounded even more absurd. "First make a small loaf from what you have and bring it to me, and then prepare the rest for you and your son. For this is what the LORD, the God of Israel, says: 'The bowl will not run out of flour or the jar out of oil'" (vv. 13-14, emphasis added).

Then the Scripture says, "The widow went and did.... and the bowl did not run out of flour nor did the jar run out of oil" (vv. 15-16).

That's tough faith—trusting God when the containers are empty. But, of course, the point is that unless they are empty, we don't need to trust. You can't have tough faith—the kind that triggers growth—until you meet God at the bottom of the empties!

I remember my first real lesson in tough faith. Thirty-one years ago, Lois and I were en route from college to seminary driving a pickup and pulling a U-Haul loaded with all our worldly possessions. We had had the first tests run on Cindy and would receive the results when we reached our destination.

A car flashed before us seemingly out of nowhere. When I awoke I was in an old house which had been converted into a small town hospital. Lois was critical. So were three from the other car. One was dead.

Two months later, our bodies had healed, but our souls were still hemorrhaging. We had lost everything we owned in the wreck. Our daughter had been pronounced mentally retarded and then upgraded to profoundly deaf.

We moved to the seminary on the first of August, paid thirty-five dollars rent on an old house, wired together what little furniture we had left, and enrolled Cindy and Lois in speech school. Then I started looking for a job. We had enough supplies to last about a month.

By the first of September, we had four dollars left, no food, and no job. We could buy milk for the baby or gas for the car.

We opted for the milk. Lois and I had never prayed together except before meals, but now we did, or rather she did. All I could do was cry. Her prayer was calm and to the point. "We're running on empty, Father. You know that. So show us what You want us to do."

The phone rang not five minutes later. I had applied for a job weighing trucks at a cottonseed oil mill a month earlier. The boss said I could have the job, but only if I could work the 8:00 P.M. to midnight shift. (He had no idea I had to attend school during the day!) Furthermore, he said, the job tended to get boring because only two or three trucks came to the mill in one shift. All I had to do was record their weight when they pulled in loaded and left empty. I should find something productive to do with my time, he said. "Like study!" I yelled under my breath.

"Lois and I had never prayed together except before meals, but now we did, or rather she did. All I could do was cry."

"One more thing," he said. "You have to start tonight. If you don't, I'll give the job to one of those preacher boys over at the Baptist seminary. There's a long line of 'em who want the job. I'd rather not hire 'em 'cause they're always trying to convert everybody. They don't steal though. You don't happen to be one of 'em, do you?"

"H_ _ _, no!" I replied. "I'll be there at eight."

On the way to the mill, I realized that we'd have to hold out until payday, but I didn't see how we could. Lois said the Lord knew about that, too, but she'd speak to Him about it.

When I asked the boss how long until payday, he said two weeks. "Look, I'm broke. I have no gas…" I told him my sad story. "This here mill's owned by Proctor and Gamble," he said. "The P&G policy is no wages in advance, period!" When I started to protest, he reminded me of the waiting list and asked if I still wanted the job. I said yes, and he walked away.

A man came up to me and said, "Pardon me, but I heard you and the boss talking." He reached into his soaked overalls and came out with a soggy bill. It had Andrew Jackson's picture on it.

"Man, you can't be making more than a dollar and a quarter an hour shoveling cottonseed," I said. "You can't afford to lend anyone twenty dollars and you don't know me at all."

"No, I cannot," he admitted. "But I have chickens and a garden. And I live in the country with my wife and kids and parents and grandparents. And what we can't grow to eat, we catch and shoot."

He paused for a moment and just looked at me. Then his eyes misted a little. "Besides," he said, "I know how a baby sounds when it cries 'cause it's hungry. There ain't no sound like it in the whole mournful world." Then my eyes misted.

But I still had to face the landlady. She looked out of the front door at Lois and me and the baby standing on the porch. "I don't carry folks," she said. We just stood there, the three of us, looking at her. "I said, I don't carry folks!" This time she said it louder. Silence again.

"Okay, two weeks," she said disgustedly. As she walked away, I heard her asking herself why she ever became a landlady. I didn't speak to her because Lois said it was all right; she'd already spoken to the Lord about the landlady. "He already knew about her, too, but I spoke to Him anyway."

Trouble triggers the kind of faith that can be experienced only when you're running on empty. I never want to go back to times like that, but if I have to, I won't be nearly as afraid.

ROUNDED CHARACTER

Trouble triggers tough faith, but toughness is not the ultimate goal of faith. James says as much. As soon as he finishes speaking of endurance, he adds, "Make sure your endurance carries you all the way with out failing, so that you may be perfect and complete, lacking in nothing" (James 1:4).

Trouble toughens us, takes away our fear, and lets us know we can stand up and take it. But trouble should take us beyond toughness to what I call rounded character. Some translators of James call it completeness; others call it perfection or full maturity. Whatever you call it, rounded character describes a person who is satisfied with what he has. "Lacking in nothing" is the goal of faith. I'm not talking about smug complacency or fully met needs. I'm talking about a lack of wanting, the kind of attitude exhibited by Dag Hammarskjöld, the first Secretary General of the United Nations. Shortly before his untimely death, he wrote a prayer in his diary:

> For all that has been, Thanks.
> For all that is yet to be, Yes!

There's nothing like trouble to round character to the point where we no longer feel the frantic wanting for more and more. "Let toughness carry you to the point where you're not driven by a sense of lacking"— that's what James is telling us to do with our suffering. Let your hurts fix your "wanters."

The Not-Easilies

In over thirty years of pastoring people in churches, I have been blessed by all kinds of people with all kinds of character, positive and negative. But the ones who have energized me most are those I call the "Not-Easilies," which is short for "Not-Easily-Offended."

The Not-Easilies forgive you when you mess up. They hold steady in rough times and have no hidden agendas. They air what few grievances they have in private and face-to-face, rather than in Bible class on Sunday morning. They are balcony people—everything's out there on the balcony for everyone to see. Almost without exception, the Not-Easilies know first-hand what it's like to hurt.

"I call them the Kingdom commandos .... They have a common brokenness because they've experienced the refining fires of moral bank-ruptcy and have developed rounded character."

Jack and Bea Holland are two of my favorite Not-Easilies. They've been loving me in spite of me for twenty years. Jack was Dean of Students at the University of Texas until he retired the first year I came to the campus church two decades ago.

When he was sixty-five, he made the motion to pull up stakes and move the entire church to a new location. When the motion was defeated, he and Bea and I and about fifty others went anyway. Now every Sabbath, Bea and Jack drive thirty miles, brave the crowds, and rejoice at all the "young 'uns" who are smothering and crowding out us old-timers.

Most of the thousands who now "sit under the trees that Jack and Bea planted" don't know that they have two kids about my age. The first was left in the birth canal too long, deprived of oxygen. Hardly more than a year later, so was the second, even though the doctors had been alerted about the problems with the first one.

You'd never know this tragic tale if you waited for Bea and Jack to tell you. The "kids," now in their fifties, are at the State School. The Hollands laugh a lot and throw a great party. Their "wanters" are fixed. Tragedy has taken them from tough faith to rounded character.

The Twelve-Steppers

I have a church full of Twelve-Steppers—people who prac-tice the Twelve Steps of Recovery developed by Alcoholics

Anonymous. The Twelve-Step program works for all addictions. We have recovering alcoholics, relatives of alcoholics, overeaters, and other addicts.

I call them the Kingdom commandos. God is revitalizing the church today by sending thousands of these people to us. The founders of A.A. took the New Testament concepts of confession, repentance, fellowship, support, works, and faith, and they stripped them of their religious language in order to get alcohol abusers to seek help. Yet even without the language, many Twelve-Step groups are "out-churching" the churches.

I can tell you this, I'll take all of them I can get. They have a common brokenness because they've experienced the refining fires of moral bankruptcy and have developed rounded character. When I mess up and confess, they say, "Okay, pastor, you've admitted your fault and taken the first step to correct it. Now it's our problem. What we think of you is no longer any of your business." They're always using quaint sayings like that.

Whenever a Twelve-Stepper says, "I don't need the church," I say, "You're probably right. But the church sure needs you."

TRUE PRAYER

So trouble can trigger tough faith, which in turn develops into rounded character which is marked by a cessation of wanting. But, of course, this is a lifetime pursuit. No one obtains perfection in the sense of wanting nothing. Eventually we all have to admit that our toughness and character are flawed; we need something more.

James knew that, too. First, he says, "Be thankful for trouble. It leads to endurance." Secondly, he says, "Let your endurance carry you to rounded character so that you lack nothing." Then he says, "but" (James 1:5).

The Greek word which is translated "but" is a word which always denotes sharp contrast. *But* means "on the other hand." James is saying, "On the other hand, when you find yourself short on character...when you really blow it and fall apart...when your tough faith becomes tenderfoot faith and your character gets 'totaled' by the wrecks of life, there is always a grace available to you. It is prayer! Pray to God. He always gives generously. But pray trusting" (James 1:5-6).

There's nothing like trouble to trigger true prayer. I use the adjective *true* because there are so many exercises that parade themselves in the name of prayer but are not.

> **"True prayer is designed to change those who pray. Prayer does not convince God to alter reality to fit me, but alters me to fit reality."**

Altered states of consciousness are not necessarily states of prayer. I've done my share of contemplative meditation. Meditation can be a very helpful tool for getting in touch with realities which go unnoticed most of the time. Have you ever listened to your own heart beat? You can hear it if you learn how. Have you ever focused on a part of your body which is in pain and localized the hurting area and isolated it and observed it objectively, and therefore conquered it? You can do this with great benefit. Meditation can also trigger inspirations that enable God to enter our souls.

And as you know, you can alter your consciousness in many other ways. Americans are the world's experts at "AC"—drugs, sports, music, etc. But you don't have to work yourself into an auto-suggestive trance in order to pray. Praying isn't trancing.

Praying isn't magic manipulation of Deity either. People still persist in the belief that prayer is designed to change God's mind, feelings, and attitudes toward the ones who are praying. Celestial begging and bargaining is still alive and well. And when our request isn't granted, we turn to professional supplicators, ones who have a "hotline": priests, preachers, and prayer lines. And if that doesn't work, we may even resort to another language altogether, one which nobody understands but God!

If you think I'm poking fun, you're dead wrong. All prayer is helpful in some way. The very fact that people recognize their need to fill the spiritual void in their lives by calling upon a reality beyond themselves has merit. Even those desperate souls who've traded God in for the zodiac aren't hopeless cases. At least they know their need to rely upon something besides themselves, even if it is something as pathetic as burning blobs called stars.

True prayer is designed to change those who pray. Prayer does not convince God to alter reality to fit me, but alters me to fit reality. James doesn't say, "Ask God to change the world to fit you." He says, "When you run out of toughness and character to face the world, ask God and He will fill you up with it!"

True prayer is an intimate visit with a trusted Father who wants to give you the grace and courage to transform your trouble into triumph. It is not an emergency call to a celestial fireman.

Blaise Pascal, who lived in the seventeenth century, knew about prayer. His *Pensées,* the French word for thoughts, remains a classic on personal devotion. He was haunted for most of his life by a need for oneness with God. One day he went to the solitude of the forest and decided to lie facedown until either he died or met God as really and personally as if he were meeting a living human.

After many hours he was almost delirious. He resigned himself to death. Then a thought burned into his consciousness: "If you did not possess me already, you would not be here seeking me."[2]

This experience had a profound effect on Pascal's devotional life. Later, after the death of his sister who was also his closest friend and after being deserted by his colleagues in science and religion, Pascal wrote, "I have lived with three great delusions in my life: The delusion that I could shape my own destiny; the delusion that I could create my own happiness; and the delusion that I could create my own security. It was out of suffering that I came to see how foolish I had been. And it was also out of suffering that I was led to know God as my trusted friend."[3]

Trouble led to tough faith, which led to rounded character, which led to true prayer when faith and character failed. Prayer changed Pascal to fit the task of transforming his trouble into triumph.

Once I did a wedding in West Texas. The marriage represented the union of two of the county's most prominent families. All stops were pulled. They sent a private plane to fetch me from Austin. The afternoon of the wedding night, the father of the bride asked if I'd like to go with him out to the airport to see the cake.

"The airport?" I said. "What's the cake doing at the airport?" "They're flyin' it in," he said, "by customized jet. The cake and the delivery cost $16,000." (And that was prior to the great inflation bump of the early seventies.)

The jet taxied up to the terminal. Doors opened and a hydraulic platform emerged with the cake perched on top. A large woman, who could've been anybody's grandmother, stood in the door of the jet directing the entire procedure. There was no doubt who was in charge. She said little. The crew obviously had done this before.

As the truck pulled out, I went over and introduced myself. "What company do you work for?" I said. "My own," she beamed.

Then she told me an amazing story. At the age of twenty-four, she was married to a truck driver and had three children. They lived in a small town in Texas. Her husband was killed, leaving her with no means of support. "All I had," she said, "was girls, guts, gumption, and God. *And* I could cook!" she bellowed, punching me in the ribs.

"I went to a wedding shortly after my husband's death," she continued. "The cake was pretty, but it tasted like cardboard. I said to myself, 'I can make cakes that taste as good as they look.'

"That's how it all started, preacher. A little old slip of a widow with nothing but girls and guts and gumption and God. Now I deliver cakes everywhere!"

Then she added, "Trouble's a trigger! Did you know that?"

3

Wait to Worry

The fear of having to face suffering is often worse than actually facing it. Human beings may be the only creatures who anticipate death and pain. This anticipation and the fear that accompanies it is called anxiety or worry.

Worry probably kills more people than the things they worry about. I know firsthand. Forty-two-year-old men who don't smoke and who run fifty miles a week rarely have clogged arteries; I did.

Several years after the surgery, I learned that the blocked artery was only 60 percent occluded and should have been treatable without opening the chest. However, my heart was in spasm, and it was literally squeezing the artery shut. I and my doctors believe that stress—the by-product of worry—was the chief culprit.

I had started my professional life over again at the age of forty-one. I resigned a large church and planted a new one with sixty people. I had one child in drug treatment, one in college, and one with chronic respiratory problems. I also had a mortgage and a salary which was only a third of what it had been.

To support my family, I started speculating in real estate,

which was booming in Texas at the time. Before I knew it, I had over a million dollars in the bank. But I owed two million dollars on land which I was holding to sell, and interest rates were hovering near 20 percent.

I had learned years before how to get by on four hours of sleep per night, and I have always worked seven days a week, just as I do now. Because I now had heavier responsibilities, I increased my exercise load in order to compensate!

But I don't think it was hard work that got to me. It was worry. I made a bad deal. To make things worse, the guy who suckered me was mega-rich with a questionable reputation. I had been warned about him, yet I went ahead. Then I turned on myself. *How could I have been so stupid?* I pondered it day and night. It turned into a full-fledged self-loathing, an obsessive self-hatred.

And I kept adding to it. For instance, I felt that I had finally proven to Dad that I could make money like the rest of the family. For the first time I was driving the same cars and making the same exotic trips. And now I was about to blow it all because I had been so incredibly stupid!

Keep in mind that I hadn't lost a dime up to that point. I still had a cool million in the bank. But I couldn't see any way to avoid the wreck which lay ahead.

WAIT TO WORRY

When I awoke from surgery, I was too cold to be in hell. (They had packed my chest cavity in ice during the procedure.) And I was too sick to be in heaven. It had to be the ICU. There and then I made a decision—I would do life differently if I survived.

A few months later, I went to a retreat where I met Fred Smith, Sr. Fred had the credentials I wanted—a successful businessman and an extraordinary Christian. He had shouldered heavy debts and was a straight-shooter. If you didn't want to know what Fred thought, you didn't ask.

I told him about my dilemma. He just sat there without expression, so I kept on talking. After several minutes, I said, "Fred, how do you deal with worry?" That finally got a rise out of him.

"I don't know when I got it," he said, "but God put a little neon sign inside my brain. Every time I get anxious about the future, it starts flashing on and off, on and off. You know what it says? 'W-T-W'— 'Wait-to-Worry.'"

That was all he had to say. When I asked him to explain, he just smirked as though I were a hopeless case.

"Wait-to-Worry" was sent straight to me from God through Fred and saved my life. What I was afraid would happen in my business did happen, but not then. In fact, I made some more millions. I even made a handsome profit off of the "bad deal" with the slicker, most of which I gave away.

The point here is that Fred started me thinking about worry in a new way. *What if I worried only when it was time to worry? Worry has mostly to do with what-if's and not-yet's and maybe's. Worry concerns the future over which we have no control.*

WHEN JESUS SAYS TO WORRY

I started trying to think of a place in the Bible that talks about worry. And to my surprise, Wait-to-Worry was precisely the approach that Jesus took. Jesus did not say, "Don't worry." We need to note that up front. To worry is altogether human. Jesus was a realist. Instead of saying "Don't worry," He said, "Wait till the proper time; then start worrying!" In Matthew 6:25, He gives us the four occasions when it's time to worry.

When It Will Feed and Clothe You

First Jesus says to worry when it will feed and clothe you.
"Consider the birds flying around," He says. "They don't plow
and sow and cultivate and harvest and store. But your heavenly Father feeds them. Flowers, too. Look at them. They don't
spin and sow, but they are clothed more beautifully than King
Solomon."

**" 'If worry will feed and clothe you,' says
Jesus, 'then worry about food and clothing.
Otherwise, wait.' "**

Then He adds, "Aren't you worth more than birds?"
(Matthew 6:26).

I've been to Africa several times. I love the bush and the
bush people. Many think of them as primitive, but I have come
to know them as a noble and wise people. One of my favorites
is our camp manager, Jeremiah. He and I have shared many a
fine African night over a campfire.

During one of our chats, I told him how impressed I was
with the fact that the bush people, who spend almost all of
their time simply trying to find food for a day, do not seem to
be anxious or driven by worry.

He smiled knowingly. "Oh, yes," he said. "And no doubt
your first thought was that perhaps the people are so primitive
that they haven't the sophistication to worry." He had me, and
he knew it. "We have a saying. ' 'Worry does not pass the
belly nor warm the back.' "

You cannot eat worry, and you cannot wear it. I thought of
the story about the guru who arrived at Grand Central Station
fresh from his mountain retreat in India. After watching the
rush for a while, he said to his host, "What's wrong with these
people? Is there a monster behind them?" "No," said the host.

"There's a dollar in front of them!"

"If worry will feed and clothe you," says Jesus, "then worry about food and clothing. Otherwise, wait."

When It Will Add to Your Life

The second proper time to worry is *when it will make you live longer or grow taller;* that is, when it will add quality or quantity to your life. Jesus asks a simple question: "Can any of you live a bit longer by worrying about it?" (Matthew 6:27). By all estimates worry never adds to life; it only diminishes it.

Have you heard the story of Willie Jones? He lived in the early 1900s when medical science was discovering and isolating germs of various kinds. A new theory about which microbe carried which disease appeared almost every month.

A wealthy man, Willie Jones loved baseball. He was also paranoid about contracting diseases from others. Like the late Howard Hughes, he hired healthy people in white sterile uniforms to care for him and fumigated his office and house regularly. At the local baseball stadium, he had his own private section and bathroom.

The story goes that one day Willie was at the game when the pitcher was throwing "spitters." He would immerse the ball in an ample amount of tobacco juice before every pitch. One of the batters fouled a line drive right at Willie. Willie couldn't duck, and he didn't want to take a direct hit, so he put out his white-gloved hands and caught the ball right in front of his face. A brownish spray engulfed him like a cloud. When he realized what it was, he dropped dead on the spot. The coroner listed the cause of death as "acute anxiety."

The following words appear on Willie's tombstone:

> Here lie the bones of Willie Jones
> For whom death held great terrors.
> He lived germ free and died germ free.
> No hits, no runs, no errors!

Of course, there never was a Willie Jones who died from the fear of tobacco spittle-spray. But people have died and will die from worries which are equally ridiculous. Jesus says, "Worry when it will add quality and quantity to your life. Otherwise, wait to worry."

When You Want to Be a Pagan

Then He gives the third proper time to worry: *when you want to know how it really feels to be a pagan.* "These are the things the pagans are always concerned about" (Matthew 6:32).

There's a lot of confusion about pagans. For instance, it is *not* true that pagans have no god; they usually have many. Once the Apostle Paul traveled to Athens. There was a hill overlooking a town which had hundreds of statues representing every god imaginable. The Greeks even erected one statue with no name on it dedicated to any god they happened to have overlooked (Acts 17:16ff).

Pagans are very religious. They have deities and ethics and intricate belief systems. They are extremely superstitious as in the case of the Athenians who were afraid of offending some god whom they hadn't discovered.

The key to understanding how a pagan feels is to imagine what it's like to have a god who is undependable—a "maybe-god." Maybe he will be there for me, or maybe he'll leave me to face the dragons alone. Maybe he'll feed me, maybe he won't. Therefore, worry is the dominant, everyday emotion of paganism. If you have a maybe-god, you will make worry your constant companion. Worry is "unfaith," not trusting your god to keep promises.

Apply this to the story of Adam and Eve. Things started going wrong when their trust in God's intentions turned to mistrust. The serpent sowed the first seed. "You won't die if you eat the fruit," he said. "God is simply trying to keep you under his thumb. He doesn't want you to be like him."

So they ate. And what was the first result? Worry. First, they became worried about being vulnerable to each other. You can almost hear them saying to themselves, "If we can't trust God, can we trust each other? Here we are naked before each other, exposed. Each of us has the power to hurt the other. Watch out!"

So they put on clothes. No longer would they be totally open to each other. Their sexuality was no longer merely a way of celebrating their love and partnering with God in the creative process. Now it was a tool of power and manipulation.

They started worrying about their work, too. Since they no longer trusted God, they would have to trust in their own labor for survival. The grinding worry about savings and pension plans and social security has its roots in a more fundamental anxiety—the worry of being without a dependable God.

Some years ago when I was "high-rolling," a major denominational magazine asked if I would do an article on financial freedom for ministers. They said they wanted twenty-five hundred words. I said I could do it in twenty-one words. "The secret of financial freedom is to be totally free of worry about finances; and you can do this without money." They didn't take the article, but I still stand by it. You cannot acquire enough money to be financially free as long as freedom means the absence of worry.

But back to Adam and Eve. Once God became untrustworthy, then came worry over dominance and work. Next came worry over offspring. Childbearing, which was intended to be a joy, now became a chore. Parents no longer saw themselves as the stewards of God's children; they were now the owners of *their* own children.

The two obvious worries that resulted from their mistrusting God were hiding from God and death.

Doesn't it seem ridiculous that Adam thought he could hide

from God? Not really. We still try.

And then there's death. Adam and Eve didn't seem to fear death until they began to mistrust God. All worry stems from our awareness of death.

"If a man die, shall he live again?" is the question behind all worrying. For example, materialism—the obsession with getting, accumulating, enjoying, and hoarding things—is usually a form of hope, an attempt to find the permanent in the temporary.

We really do need to hear Jesus saying, "If you want to know how it feels to be a pagan—to be forced to trust in your own wiles because your god cannot be trusted—then worry. But if you have a God who is a loving Father and knows what you need and can be trusted to meet your needs (not wants), then wait to worry."

I told you that when I awoke from surgery I decided to do life differently. I didn't know what that meant exactly. In the ten years since, I have learned to ask myself the question: "Wherein lies your ultimate security?" Or more simply: "Who do you trust—not for your wants, but for your needs?" I've had my best days when I've answered, "Your Father in heaven knows what you need" (Matthew 6:32).

> **"Adam and Eve didn't seem to fear death**
> **until they began to mistrust God.**
> **All worry stems from our awareness**
> **of death."**

When You Want Tomorrow to Be Worse

So Jesus tells us to worry: (1) when worry will feed and clothe us; (2) when worry will add quality and quantity to life; and (3) when we want to live like the pagans.

Then He adds a fourth legitimate time for worrying: *Worry when you want tomorrow to be worse than it's already going to be.* "So do not worry about tomorrow. It will have enough worries of its own. There is no need to add to the troubles each day brings" (Matthew 6:34).

How often have you heard or said, "Don't worry! Everything's gonna turn out okay"? Jesus said, "Don't worry! Everything's *not* gonna turn out okay! In fact, a good portion of it will turn out *not okay.* Tomorrow will be filled with troubles. If you want to make them worse than they're already gonna be, then add the dimension of worry to them today. That way you can be miserable now as well as then!"

If you're happily married and intend to stay that way, there are some dark days ahead. Most likely, one of you will have to bury the other and live alone for an average of sixteen years, according to statistics. Want to make it worse? Worry about it now! If you want to take away the joy of a good marriage, worry! Is your pension shrinking? Yes. If it's not, Congress will raid it. If you want to make things worse, worry about it.

Will your child make it through life according to your dream? Nope. Make it worse. Worry!

Does this sound cynical? Jesus says, "Be concerned above everything else with the kingdom of God and with what he requires of you, and he will provide you with all these other things" (Matthew 6:33). We're to worry about God's wants, not our needs. He'll take care of our needs if we will take care of His wants.

A friend of thirty years called long distance. "All hell's about to break loose," he sobbed. He was one of the state's most prominent citizens. As a young man, he started a small business and built it into a corporate empire. He had a model family. Charities had received liberal donations. Employees shared in the profits of the company. Fifty cents of every dollar he made was given away or shared.

"Tomorrow I will be indicted for tax fraud," he said. "To tell you the truth, I don't know whether I'm legally guilty. I made a lot of money. I told the accountants to avoid all of the taxes they could. We may have crossed the line between avoidance and evasion. I can't honestly say."

He paused for a long moment. "But I can say this, Gerald. I cannot bear to expose my family to this disgrace. My wife and children are suspicious of me for the first time. I'm sitting here with a gun in my lap. I don't know whether I should do it now or after the story hits the papers. My world has ended."

I knew he was crying out for help; otherwise he wouldn't have called. He would have simply pulled the trigger. The wrong word would have been disastrous. But what was the correct word? My mind screamed for an answer. Then the words just flowed out like water. "No, it hasn't," I demanded. "You feel too d _ _ _ bad for it to be the end of the world!"

"Don't get cute," he replied. "You don't know how I feel!"

"Yes, I do. You feel awful. You feel trapped. You don't think you can make it. You can see the shame, the scandal, the jokes, the tears. Well, the Bible says when the end comes, it's going to be trumpets and angels and choirs and wonders.

"Your world hasn't ended. A chapter of your life has. And the only word I get from God is, wait to worry! Did you hear me?" I waited.

"Okay. I'll say it again: wait to worry! Wait until they indict you. Wait till you get a lawyer. Then wait till you get his bill. Wait till you're pronounced guilty. Wait for the sentencing. Wait for the cell door to close. But wait to worry."

"Many of the troubles which paralyze us
are the ones that never happen."

He was indicted and went to trial. He paid gigantic legal fees. But two years later he was exonerated and acquitted of all charges.

I saw him a while back at a political campaign function. He saw me, ran across the room, and hugged me. "I want you to know that your three words saved my life," he said. "I have them posted everywhere. In my car, on the refrigerator, on my desk. All over the offices. What I've learned is that God is out there in the future waiting for us."

"'Wait to Worry' are not my three words," I replied. "They're God's. He gave 'em to Fred who gave 'em to me who gave 'em to you."

Many of the troubles which paralyze us are the ones that never happen. The fear of having to suffer is as crippling as facing the suffering itself. We cannot avoid that fear. To worry is human. But we can wait until it's time to worry. We can get that little neon sign going inside our brains and let it flash every time our insides knot up over the what-if's and not-yet's and maybe's.

4

Ruts Ain't Roots

The bad times cannot be over for good as long as we confuse ruts with roots. Roots are the deep sources from which we draw strength. Ruts are the deep grooves left by our predecessors that choke off life.

I learned to drive in the Brazos River bottoms where the average annual rainfall was forty-eight inches. If you drove at all, you drove on muddy roads. The cardinal rule of driving in the mud was "Stay in the ruts!" You held the wheel loosely enough to allow the wheels to turn with the ruts, yet firmly enough to keep them from jumping out of the ruts.

We do life the same way, until, of course, the ruts run us into the bog.

The root of a healthy marriage is spontaneity and mystery. When people ask me the secret of our thirty-three years together, I always answer, "Whoopee!" and "For-the-h _ _ _-of-it."

"Whoopee!" stands for creative celebration, creative discussion, creative lovemaking, creative everything. We never try anything the same way twice if we can think of another way to do it.

"For-the-h _ _ _-of-it" means, *for no good reason.* I buy her roses two weeks *after* our anniversary. They're delivered to the house, and the card says, "For-the-h _ _ _-of-it." We do most everything on the spur of the moment.

Spontaneity, mystery, creative caring form the root of a great relationship. Nevertheless, we keep trying to trade it in for the same old, same old. I saw a couple at dinner the other evening. They came in, ordered, drank, ate, burped, and left with only three grunts exchanged between them.

Ruts ain't roots. Nowhere do we forget this more than in religion. There are three fundamental roots that vitalize the Christian faith and are the essential life-giving sources for transforming trouble into triumph. There are certainly other roots which nourish religion, but without these three, religion isn't much good when tragedy comes calling.

Yet we religious people have a tendency to trade these roots for ruts. Consequently, when suffering strikes, we have no weapons with which to fight.

Paul wrote a letter to Christian believers in Corinth, the bustling prosperous seaport in southern Greece. The church at Corinth had confused ruts with roots. When Paul first introduced them to Christ, they had flourished. Although they lived in the cradle of pagan culture, they had won many converts. But within a few short years, they had managed to install traditions and practices—ruts—that had made them powerless. From a vital force for Christ they had quickly become an ignored cult in much the same way that many churches are ignored today.

Paul is calling the Corinthians back to their roots in his letter. In Chapter 15, he lays out the three roots which give power to those called Christians.

> I want to remind you. I want to call you back to the basics of the Good News which I first preached to you, which you received, and on which your faith rests. You are made whole [saved] by this Good News unless your

beliefs become rutted in nothing. (1 Corinthians 15: 1-2, author's translation)

The Corinthians had severed their roots. They had turned Good News faith into bad news religion. The great flaw of all Christian movements is that they cut the roots which give them life and fall into the ruts which make people worship themselves.

Let's look at the roots we must have to live and the ruts we choose instead.

"The great flaw of all Christian movements is that they cut the roots which give them life and fall into the ruts which make people worship themselves."

THE ROOT OF REPRIEVE

We hear and read a lot about forgiveness. But when I think of God's forgiveness, I use a stronger word: *Reprieve.* More than the forgiveness of an offense, a reprieve is also the cancellation of the penalty that goes with it. You're guilty and you've been caught red-handed. But a higher authority cancels the penalty and pronounces you innocent.

Religion is of no practical value if it cannot connect people with reprieve. People need to feel innocent again, not merely forgiven.

"Christ died for our sins" (1 Corinthians 15:3). That means a reprieve for you and for all of us. Has the phrase "Christ died for our sins" ever confused you? Back in preacher school, we studied volumes on its meaning, but I was as confused when I finished as when I started.

One theory was that Jesus died on the Cross to ransom us from the devil, as if we or God owed the devil anything. Another theory was that Jesus died as a payoff to the righteous part of God's nature. God is so absolutely pure that He can't allow sin to go unpunished so Jesus died to satisfy God's "anger," as if God were a prisoner to His own emotions and couldn't simply let us off by His own will.

The phrase, "Christ died for our sins" means two things to me. First, He's done all of the dying that ever needs to be done. Second, God has shouldered His responsibility for creating a world where things went wrong. There are two great traditions in Christian thought about the original humans and why they broke relationship with God. One stems from Augustine and the other from Irenaeus.

Augustine (A.D. 354-430) believed that Adam and Eve were created perfect but with the freedom to reject God. God didn't want robots to love Him. He wanted free relationships. Adam and Eve chose to worship the created instead of the Creator.

Irenaeus (A.D. 130-202), who wrote the first systematic theology for Christianity, took a different approach.[1] How could Adam and Eve have been perfect and in total union with God, and then chosen to break with Him? They couldn't have been perfect, said Irenaeus. They were created at a "distance" from God—innocent like children but not fully matured. He used the Greek translation of Genesis 1:26 ("Let us make man in our image, and after our likeness") to support his argument that Adam was created imperfect but with the potential ("image") to grow to godly perfection ("likeness").

Whether you follow the Augustinian or Irenaean tradition, you end up at the Cross, where God took the responsibility for creating a world where things went wrong. The good news of the Cross is that *we know a great secret!* No more dying ever has to be done! God is out to win us all. The only difference between a Christian and a non-Christian is that the Christian knows the secret and has accepted God's gracious gift. As Carlyle Marney used to say, "We know everybody's real name. It's Jesus. Jesus is the name of our species."[2]

Reprieve is written across the title page of every human life. Christ died for us all.

Anytime you talk about reprieve, you're faced with the question of "second chances beyond the grave." Many people grieve over loved ones who have died without expressing any faith or allegiance to God.

I want to speak a word of encouragement to you. I think that God, being the kind of God He is, would continue to pursue a relationship with us beyond this life. No, I do not have a single verse of Scripture to support this possibility. On the contrary, the biblical material indicates that our choices for eternity are made in this life.

My feeling is based on the character of God as revealed in the entire body of Scripture. God relentlessly seeks to be reunited with His people. No matter how many times they break their promises to Him, He keeps His to them. The Cross is the proof of the extremes God will pursue to win us.

He won't overrule our free choice to reject Him in this life or the next, which makes hell a reality and one we choose for ourselves. But I wouldn't be surprised to find God still reaching out to people in the next life.

Obviously this is speculation, but it's based on the love of God. I know one thing for sure: It's okay with me if God keeps trying. I believe in justice, that no evil is unpunished. But standing over against the most radical evil is the more radical love of God that says, "Christ died for our sins," and that spells reprieve.

> *"Reprieve is written across the title page of every human life."*

My sister was involved in a freak accident at the age of twenty-nine. A truck loaded with ammonia fell from an upper to a lower level of a freeway interchange and exploded. She was trapped in the ensuing traffic pileup and inhaled the corrosive gas.

For fifteen years, she has lived with burned and infected lungs. As she neared death a few months ago, she had to decide whether to go on life support. This was not the case of an elderly person vegetating in a comatose state. She was in full control of her faculties. To refuse the respirator meant literally smothering to death while fully conscious.

We talked. She said, "I must ask you something, and I want an answer I can understand. How can I know that I'm okay with God when I die?"

"Because you want to be," I answered. "But you've forgotten the things I used to do!" she protested. "No, I haven't forgotten," I said. "But God has!" The Bible not only says that God forgives our sins; it also says, "He remembers them no more." God is absentminded about our past, even though we aren't.

She still had a burden to unload. "There's something you don't know about," she said. "Just before the accident years ago, we were in awful financial shape. I thought we were going to lose everything. One day I thought, *What if we had an accident and could sue for huge damages? Our troubles would be over.*"

She choked up and said, "The next day I had the accident. We received a huge settlement. Now it's all gone for medical bills, and I'm dying. Do you think God has been punishing me for all of these years? And will I still be punished after I die?"

I was crying, too. "What kind of God would burn the lungs of a desperate young person who fantasized financial rescue through a lawsuit!" I said.

"What if you'd fantasized the rescue by winning the lottery?

Or the Publishers' Clearinghouse Sweepstakes? I paste those stamps on Ed McMahon's face every year myself! In fact, I'm counting on winning as the one thing that will rescue me from bankruptcy!"

I read to her 1 John 1:9: "If we confess our sins to God, we can depend on Him. He will forgive our sins and cleanse (which means, *to erase, wipe out*) all of our dirtiness" (author's translation).

THE RUT OF RETRIBUTION

Through fifteen years of coughing up infected sputum and fighting for breath and praying to God for health, this tortured soul had not connected with the first root of the Good News: *Reprieve.* "Christ died for our sins." That's because she had fallen into the rut of retribution.

Many Christians have traded the root of reprieve for the rut of retribution. In a thousand subtle ways we repeat the big lie of the serpent: "God really can't be your friend. He only wants to keep you captive. Don't believe for a minute that He's a loving Father. If you don't watch out, He'll get you."

The threat of retribution is a convenient tool of power for religious practitioners. It's not lost on parents either. Have you ever analyzed the words of the most famous Santa Claus song children sing at Christmas? "Oh, you better watch out! You'd better not cry! You'd better be good. I'm tellin' you why . . . He's makin' a list . . . Checking it twice . . . naughty or nice . . . knows when you are sleeping . . . knows when you're awake . . . good or bad . . . ."

If I can get you to believe that Santa-God is "coming to town" and I know his schedule, I can get you to do all sorts of things for me. There's power in hellfire and brimstone, power for me.

But there's no power for making the bad times over for the good. The power to transform trouble lies in the life-giving root of reprieve.

John Killinger said that Jesus came into the world to cure God of a bad reputation.[3] He meant that Jesus came to erase once and for all the image of an angry God. The most revolutionary thing Jesus ever said about God was the one word *Father.* Up to that time, God had been called by many names, but never Father.

The reason you can't transform trouble into triumph with a retributive God is because you can't love Him. You can respect and fear and obey an angry God, but you cannot love Him. Love can neither occur nor endure under threat.

This is especially true where God is concerned. How can we love someone who will withdraw His love if we perform poorly? Yet we continue to hear a message of retribution from so-called Christian quarters. We continue to trade in the root of reprieve for the rut of retribution. When someone suggests that God is a loving Father who intends to bring all of His children back to Him, those who have lived for so long under the threat of retribution cannot stand it. They cannot bear the thought of God letting "sinners" off. How dare God be a Father who throws a party for wastrels!

Now you know why so many believers are paralyzed by suffering. The instant something goes wrong, they say, "What have I done wrong? What did I do to make God angry enough to visit me with this misery?" My poor sister was in exactly this trap. She thought she'd angered a retributive God. All of those years of battling to stay alive and all she had to rely on spiritually was a God she respected and feared but couldn't love.

By the way two days after our visit, she decided to go on life support. It was not out of desperation, however, but out of a quiet confidence that a loving God was with her, had always been with her, and would always be with her. She would put herself on the waiting list for a double lung transplant and trust God.

To be honest, I thought it was a mistake. But in less than a week, she moved from thirtieth on the waiting list to an almost perfect donor match and to a transplant. She is four months into her new life as I write this. Having defied the prognosis of doctors and yours truly, she is at home and living a relatively normal life.

Lung transplant patients are critically ill throughout their lives. She could do well for a lengthy period or for one day, and then it could be over in a moment.

I spoke with her recently. "You wouldn't believe how wonderful life is," she said. "Things that didn't matter, do, and things that did, don't."

"Tell me about God," I said. "Oh, well now, God," she said. "How shall I put it? He likes me a lot!"

THE ROOT OF RESURRECTION

A religion that cannot offer people a reprieve from their past is worth less. The same goes for a religion which cannot offer something better in the next life than what they can experience in this one.

So, the second root of vital faith is resurrection. "Christ died for our sins...he was buried and...he was raised to life three days later" (1 Corinthians 15:3-4).

By now you should know that my religious bias is pretty much "this worldly." I believe that religion is primarily a power for living in the now. But I must tell you that there are some things in this world which only the resurrection from the dead can fix. There's a line from John Masefield's "The Widow in the Bye Street" that I keep with me. A young man is being publicly hanged for so-called crimes against the state. His widowed mother is standing in the crowd. When the trap is released, she is heard to mutter something about "broken things too broke to mend." Indeed, there are "broken things too broke to mend" this side of the resurrection.

I know a minister in the Seattle area who has buried eleven boys between the ages of eight and twelve. All were cast-aways, runaways, and stolen-aways made into prostitutes for homosexuals. They all died of AIDS. Only a resurrection can rectify such horror.

I preached for a week in Georgia years ago. Near the church was a rehabilitation center for crippled children. On the first day I went for a visit and met Tommy. Six years old, he had no known surname. He had been abandoned on the doorstep of the rehab hospital as an infant. His arms and legs were stubs. The doctors surmised that his mother had taken a drug called Thalidomide which relieved complications during pregnancy.

I fell in love with Tommy. He had big blue eyes and blond ringlets. Every day I visited him. On the last day of my time there, he asked if I would return the following day. I told him I had to go home to Texas to see my little girl who had hair and eyes like his. The look on his face told me that I was another in a long line of would-be friends who had loved him and deserted him. He put his stubs around my neck and asked if he could go with me.

"A religion that cannot offer people a reprieve from their past is worthless."

I left ashamed and embittered. I shall never forget how Tommy looked at me.

There are some things too broke to mend without a resurrection. Paul thought so, too. Later, in the same chapter he says, "If Christ has not been raised from the dead, your faith is a delusion . . . . If our hope is in this life only, then we deserve more pity than anyone else in all the world" (1 Corinthians 15:17, 19).

Do you ever speculate about what you're going to do when you get to heaven? I know that the afterlife can be described only by symbols and images. We are locked in the space and time dimension with space-time language.

Lois and I have often played the "what-I'm-gonna-do-when-I-get-to heaven" game. We get funny sometimes. Lois says the first thing she's going to do is get an angel to do the ironing. The first thing I'm going to do is have all of those electric hand dryers you see in public bathrooms thrown into hell!

But sometimes we get serious. We both agree that the first thing we're going to do is gather the immediate family—us and the three children—and have the first conversation where everyone can hear and understand each other.

Some things can't be fixed without a resurrection. I want to see Cindy's face the first time she hears music and the sound of laughter and jokes and symphonies and choirs and my voice and her voice and the voice of her own child.

Sounds maudlin, I suppose. I don't care if it does. The root which gives us the nerve to transform trouble into triumph is the inner voice of God which says, "There's more to come."

THE RUT OF INSTANT GRATIFICATION

Such talk of the next life sounds strange in modern America. We have traded the root of resurrection for the rut of instant gratification. I suppose it is because life in America is a lot more "user-friendly" than it was a couple of generations ago. My grandmother lost three babies to simple diarrhea. A quart of Kaopectate would have saved a whole neighborhood.

She talked a lot about the next life, looked forward to it as a matter of fact. Hardly a day passed that she didn't tell me, "This world is not my home."

Things are different now. We've traded resurrection for instant gratification. American culture has embraced the denial of death. We have camouflaged our language. We say people "passed away." We speak of "the deceased," the "memorial park," and "interment." The fitness, flat belly, face-lift world has the faint odor of the fear of death.

Elizabeth Kübler-Ross, of near-death experiences fame, came to our church. The crowd that packed the place included those who "never darken the door." I realized that her appeal lay in the fact that she and others who speak of near-death experiences are offering people immortality at bargain-basement prices. They claim to have scientific proof that life after death is wonderful and has no connection, moral or other-wise, to how we live our lives now.

"People want fast-food faith for instant gratification more than they want any-thing else the church has to offer."

As the pastor of a large church which is noticed in national magazines for its success in reaching Baby Boomers, I must tell you that people want fast-food faith for instant gratification more than they want anything else the church has to offer. All I have to do to reduce attendance is preach three straight Sundays on commitment—giving time, talents, and treasure to a cause for which you will receive no immediate rewards. And all I have to do to refill the place is preach a series on "getting the most out of" something—your marriage, your prayers, your boss, your job.

Most Sundays we have as many visitors as members present. Some have been "visiting" for five years. They don't join because they'll be asked to give money and time and talent.

The greatest temptation of my life as a minister is a new kind of adultery—an adulteration of the Christian's call to commitment. I want to be so successful that I adulterate the Christian call to commitment for the sake of drawing big crowds.

So, why don't I run all the freeloaders off? I hope it's because I believe that they can grow past instant gratification into resurrection. I pray that eventually I can surprise them with the gospel when they're not looking.

What does that mean? I hope that after they've been loved and accepted and restored that they will decide to die so that they may live—die to their fear of death, to their stuff, to their this-world games—and be born to eternal life. Not immortality, mind you. But God's kind of life.

So I become all things to all Baby Boomers in order that I may win some. I keep on trying to jog them out of the rut of instant gratification and connect them to the root of resurrection.

There are many critics of this approach. Most of them are church analysts instead of pastors. I'd invite them into the pastorate, but they're too smart to come. Nevertheless, their criticism is accurate. The church or the individual who thinks that all needs will be glorified now by following Christ is confusing ruts with roots.

I love Alexander Solzhenitsyn's acerbic commentaries on Western culture. He is a prophet in the finest of the Old Testament traditions. He says things like, "If man were born to be happy on this earth, he wouldn't be born to die." He laments the fall of Communism in Russia (the brutal system which robbed him of his freedom for most of his adult life), if it is going to be traded in for the decadent materialism of the United States.

Solzhenitsyn is no longer in great demand on the speaker's circuit, because he reminds us that humans are not the crowning glory of the universe with no Supreme Being above them and that personal material satisfaction is not the supreme moral authority. Everything is not good simply because it preserves our economic well-being.

In a word, Solzhenitsyn is reminding us of what he discovered the hard way in the Gulag. Namely, that our highest and best end is not the rut of instant gratification but the root of resurrection.

THE ROOT OF RECOGNIZABLE REALITY

The third root which vitalizes faith is Paul's most repeated "last line of defense"—the source he fell back on whenever he was cornered. He used it when he stood before judges and prosecutors, and he uses it in his letter to the Corinthians.

This linchpin of Paul's faith was his firsthand personal encounter with the living Christ. He knew God other than by hearsay. God was a *recognizable reality.* Listen to the flow of Paul's message: First he says, "Christ died for our sins." Second, "God raised Him from the dead." Then, "I met Him! First He appeared to Peter and the apostles. Then He appeared to over five hundred of His followers. Finally He appeared to me" (1 Corinthians 15:5-8, author's translation).

God is a recognizable reality! You can know Him! That's the bottom line, the taproot of religion. A religion which cannot introduce people to a recognizable God is of no value when the roof falls in on their lives.

I am often asked, most often by other Baptists, why in the world I and our church remain Baptist. I don't talk like a Baptist preacher, and heaven knows they'd never miss us.

I give two answers. One I stole from Stephen Brown, a Presbyterian minister who's written a book on grace.[4] Steve pastors down in the Miami area. He says that Miami's ecclesiastical picture is like a grid with different shaped holes. Round folks go to the round church; square folks go to the square church; rectangular folks go to another. "Those who are left over go to our church," says Steve.[5]

I think we remain Baptists so that the leftovers will have a place.

The second reason I remain a Baptist is the real reason. I want to remain connected to a body which, in spite of its warts and pimples, insists that God has no grandchildren, that each of us must come to know God as a personal, recognizable reality.

We were finished having children. Cindy was sixteen with her many problems. Stacey was eleven and on the edge of puberty. We were only in our mid-thirties with a lot of living to do when the nest emptied.

Then came J.J., our son. Lois developed a condition called polyhydramnios in her sixth month of pregnancy. She literally swelled up with an overabundance of amniotic fluid, which indicated that some thing was wrong with the fetus.

J.J. was born two months early and weighed less than three pounds. The doctor came out of the delivery room and told me there was little chance. They couldn't get him to breathe, and even if they could, his respiratory system was malformed. Most likely he had only one lung, and it was not fully developed.

We had just moved to a new pastorate in Austin, a campus church renown for its liberalism in a positive sense, an evangelical church with a social conscience. I thought I'd come home to nirvana.

Not so. The church was a dead community living in the past. Once it had led the march for civil rights and racial justice in the fifties and sixties, but like most protest churches, it lived on nostalgic memories.

I was growth-oriented. They were not. It was oil and water.

The practical result was, on that Saturday morning in a strange new town, in the hospital with a dying son, I was alone. I had no friends to call.

I locked myself in the bathroom near the hospital waiting room. I sat the only place there was to sit. "D- - -you, God!" I said. "I've taken all of this I'm going to. No more! First a deaf one. Now, either a dead one or a severely handicapped one!"

I called God every name I learned in the locker rooms from junior high to the Southwest Conference. I wanted to die. I deserved to die and no one was going to deprive me of it!

After a while, I was exhausted. I had said all of the words and shed all of the tears.

A strange peace came over me as I sat on that toilet. *You have fought a good fight,* a thought said to me inside my head. *Now there is laid up for you the prize which the Lord will give you on that day* (2 Timothy 4:7-8).

What a weird thought for someone who had just finished cursing God! The Transactional Analysis folks have given us some neat ways to think of how we operate psychologically. The most disturbed folks operate from the feeling that "*It's* not okay," which means that all of reality is gone wrong. Conversely, the healthiest people operate out of the feeling that "It *is* okay."

In the bathroom that day, I knew "*It* was okay." God had given me another fleeting glimpse of Himself. I could transform this trouble. I could face it, fight it, and form it. How? I had no idea. But *It* was okay.

The doctors called in a pediatric surgeon who opened J.J.'s chest. He had two lungs after all, but they were collapsed by fluid buildup. For sixty days they fought to save him. They opened his chest seven more times, popping a lung once.

Do you know what apnea attacks are? That's when infants simply quit breathing. J.J. had apnea attacks for the first three months of his life. They rigged him with an alarm, and if he failed to breathe for ten seconds, the alarm would sound.

Can you imagine what it's like to bring a child home and try to sleep knowing that sometime during the night, you will have to prick him with a needle to get him to resume breathing?

Well, I couldn't if I hadn't been there. Yet all through the ordeal of that first year, I held my head into the wind. I had already endured the tempest.

By the way, J.J. made quite a running back. I smile every time I think of him, because I know God smiles every time He thinks of me giving Him a good "cussing" in the bathroom. I'm not okay, and you're not okay. But *it's* okay.

How do we know? Because we know God other than by hearsay. The taproot of our faith is a recognizable reality.

THE RUT OF REPETITIVE RITUAL

The root of a recognizable God somehow keeps getting traded for the rut of empty motions which we call rituals. We have good motives. We want to package our religious experiences in a form which will help others meet God personally and help us experience God as we did at first.

Rituals are necessary to living. We must have ways to relive what's happened between God and us in the past. No religion can last without rituals.

No relationship can endure without rituals, either. Spouses and families and friendships have certain rituals without which their relationships would die.

Lois and I have a ritual that Charlie Shedd, the great Presbyterian author and now my teammate at our church, gave us years ago. We have a talk a day. For thirty minutes, we unplug the phone and lock the door. Nothing interferes.

We have a date a week. We leave the house, kids, everything

to be exclusively with each other. And we have a "whoopee a month"—an overnight away from home.

Religion needs rituals, too. We need symbols and routines that remind us visually of the moments when God intersected our lives and the lives of our forefathers. But here's the problem: We tend to substitute the ritual for the reality. Typically, we encounter God and then build "boxes" for remembering the encounter and repeating it. Then we end up worshipping the "boxes" God came in, instead of God Himself.

Kris Kristofferson, the songwriter and actor, had an experience which exemplifies how we trade in the root of a knowable God for the rut of ritual.

This story was told to me by my friend Larry Gatlin, another singing star. Larry said he took Kris to church with him, an evangelical church that gave an altar call at the end of each service. People who want to publicly declare their faith in Christ are invited to come forward.

Kris had a remarkable experience with God and went forward. Gatlin says he has no doubt that the experience was real. Kristofferson went home and wrote a great song about his experience entitled "Why Me, Lord?" If you've heard it and if you've encountered God firsthand, then you suspect Kris met the real thing.

Before long Kris wanted to know more about these people who called themselves Christians. So he started hanging out with them.

Right away, Kris's life-style was called into question. He was told he could not pursue his entertainment career and be a "true witness." Gatlin says Kris soon wrote another song which didn't become famous but was just as heartfelt entitled "Me and Jesus Got Our Own Thing Goin'." Kris parted company with organized religion.

Well-meaning souls sometimes confuse the root of a recognizable God with the rut of moralistic ritual. God touches someone in our midst almost in spite of our ruts, but they can't stay.

I have tried to show that trouble can be transformed only if the three roots of reprieve and resurrection and recognizable reality remain intact.

- People can surpass their past if they can breathe the clean air of God's forgiveness and forgetfulness of their past.
- People can endure the most hideous, absurd evils if they know there's resurrection, if they know that beyond this life there's more life.
- People can transform trouble into triumph if the substance of their faith is a recognizable present-and-accounted-for God.

But they cannot transform trouble as long as they are mired in the ruts of retribution, instant gratification, and empty ritual.

5

Miracles Happen
in Miracle Territory

Years of helping people who are immersed in suffering have made me believe in miracles. I don't mean the kind of miracles that defy so-called natural law. I have no particular problem believing that these occur. I believe that Jesus died, and I believe God raised Him from the dead. If you can believe that, you can believe the report of other events which defy our understanding of physics.

Besides, what is natural law? It is the sum total of what we understand about how the world *we think we're observing* works. There may be more to learn about what we now consider to be supernatural. It is also conceivable that our seeing mechanism alters reality. In other words, we must have faith that what we observe is actually as it appears.

To me the whole discussion of the miraculous needs to go beyond the categories of natural versus supernatural. A miracle happens any time (1) God is involved directly and personally in someone's life, (2) they recognize His presence, and (3) they do life radically differently as a result.

I have witnessed many miracles of this type. I've seen self-ish people become generous, and cowardly people become brave, liars become truthful, and haters become lovers.

Miracles do, in fact, defy "natural law" when it comes to human nature. If someday we discover that there are natural explanations for everything Jesus is reported to have done in the Bible, that's fine with me. The long history of human knowledge is our ever-increasing understanding of things that formerly were considered divine mysteries.

I have no fear that the scientific method will erase God from the human heart. The opposite is true. The very order and symmetry of the world is miraculous to me. How could any-one look at the harmony and synchronization of nature and not be awed?

My point is that our problem with miracles is not whether they defy or can be explained by natural law. *The problem is that miracles happen only in miracle territory.*

Many people never experience miracles because they don't put themselves where miracles occur. Why should God get involved in doing for us what we can do for ourselves?

Ever hear of Homer Dodge? He was an adventurer who tra-versed Antarctica and the Amazon Basin. He lived alone in the Sahara Desert. When he was past eighty, he was the last person to run the Long Salt Rapids of the St. Lawrence River in an open canoe. No one had done it since the early fur trap-pers. The St. Lawrence was dammed shortly after Dodge's great feat.

When a reporter asked him to what he attributed his long and interesting life, he said, "If you want interesting things to hap-pen to you, you must put yourself where interesting things happen." Then he added, "I've seen miracles in my life because I've always tried to place myself where miracles can happen."

I have always remembered Dr. Dodge's words. Whenever I

have taken them to heart and put them to the test, I have seen miracles.

For instance, I read once that in Africa there was a group of early Afrikaners who enjoyed rhino dodging. The rhinoceros was one of the most feared beasts of the bush because he didn't see well and tended to aim his two-ton body and sabre-like horn at anything that moved.

Years later, when I was on safari, I asked my guide about rhino dodging. "Ya," he said, "they used to do it, the bloody fools." "I want to do it," I announced.

To make a long story short, we received a rhino report one day while we were in camp. There was a rhino on a private ranch just across the border in South Africa. I could play matador with him if I liked.

We got to the place, and there he was, minding his own business, browsing along in a grassy meadow. We circled downwind.

"Many people never experience miracles because they don't put themselves where miracles occur."

The plan was to get within a hundred yards and then walk straight toward him until he saw me. Then I was going to challenge him. When he charged, I was told to wait until he was almost upon me and then dash to one side at a ninety-degree angle. The beast was so large that he couldn't turn quickly enough to skewer me on his massive horn.

We started our circle downwind until we were perhaps three hundred yards from him. We stopped. I turned to speak to the trackers. They had vanished.

I swallowed hard and started walking slowly toward the rhino. Now he was two hundred yards away and still had not seen me. It seemed like forever. My heart pounding, my mouth dry, at about a hundred yards, the beast stopped eating and raised his head.

I froze. He stared at me for a long time. The moment had come. It was time for me to challenge him. I made ready to run straight at him and shout. And I made ready…and I made ready. My legs would not obey my brain. They absolutely rebelled.

I never got to dodge a charging rhino. After what seemed an eternity, the monster simply resumed his munching. I quietly retreated on my hands and knees, hoping not to soil my trousers.

But if you would ever like to experience the exhilaration of dodging a rhino, I can provide you with some expert data.

First, you can't dodge rhinos in Detroit. You have to go where there are rhinos. Second, you have to find one. Third, you have to put yourself in front of him. And finally, you must have the bowels to challenge him. I'm an expert on rhino dodging although I've never dodged one.

Well, I enjoyed telling the story whether you got the point or I made it. You can't experience miracles unless you put yourself where they occur—beyond the limits of your self-sufficiency. I never experienced rhino dodging because I didn't venture beyond my limits. I had the nerve to look for and find the beast, and the nerve to get within a few yards of him. But I didn't push to the edge. I can tell you how a rhino smells. I can tell you how those tick birds who ride on his back look and sound.

I suspect many believers are that way when it comes to miracles. They are experts without the experience.

Which brings up the big question: How do we place ourselves in miracle territory? Miracles happen whether we see them or not.

For years, I had read the eleventh chapter of Hebrews, the "Roll Call of Faith." If you've read it, you know that the writer's aim is to strengthen the backbones of the early Jewish Christians who are under oppression from several quarters.

He sets out to define what is true faith in God. But instead of an intellectual discussion, he simply describes the heroes of biblical history. "Faith is Abel doing this and Enoch doing that." In other words, the best way to define *faith* is to show examples enacted by people who trusted in God.

As I said, I had read this chapter for years before it occurred to me that there was one thing all of these heroes had in common. They all put themselves in miracle territory, beyond the limits of their self-sufficiency. That's why they experienced miracles.

More than that, they all endured their fair share of suffering. The miracles they experienced were mostly miracles of transcending trouble and transforming it into triumph.

We're going to look at four of these heroes. Each one exemplifies how we place ourselves in miracle territory.

PERFORM BEFORE THE STORM

Noah moved into miracle territory by building a boat in the desert, miles from the nearest water. God told him a flood was coming and that evil would be destroyed.

So Noah obeyed God even though there wasn't a cloud in the sky. *You are in miracle territory when you perform before the storm.*

To perform before the storm simply means to refuse to buy into the lies which every culture tells itself. Every society eventually makes gods of its own selfish values, worshipping projected images of itself—its creeds, politics, possessions, race, nationality.

Evil is worshipping projected images of ourselves and calling them God. In pursuing these gods, we have to constantly tell ourselves lies. And therein lies the self-destructive aspect of all evil.

"The people who are able to transform trouble into triumph are the ones who build their boats before it rains."

Charles Beard, the Yale historian, was asked what he had learned in his fifty years of reading and teaching history. He said, four things:[1] (1) Whom the gods would destroy, they first make mad with power; (2) the mills of God grind slowly, but they grind exceeding small; (3) the bee always fertilizes the flower it robs; and (4) only when it's darkest do the stars come out.

Evil carries the seeds of its own destruction—that is the theme of all of the lessons Dr. Beard learned in his lifelong study.

People who know this and refuse to be taken in by the lies that are necessary to maintain evil are putting themselves in miracle territory. To perform—obey God—before the storm— before calamity strikes—is to become a candidate for the miraculous.

The people who are able to transform trouble into triumph are the ones who build their boats before it rains. They know about prayer and decency and common courtesy and goodwill long before it thunders. God is no stranger to them when the winds begin to blow.

Denton Cooley, the great heart surgeon, tells of how he trained himself to perform delicate operations. As a young intern, he spent hours each day tying knots with suture string inside an empty box which was made for kitchen matches.

He would jam his long fingers (he was a star college basket-ball player well over six feet tall) into the match box and tie those knots.

"I learned a valuable lesson which would stand me in good stead throughout my life," he said. *"He who learns to do simple things perfectly will acquire the ability to do difficult things easily."*[2]

Noah did simple things perfectly. He simply stuck to God's promises while the rest of the world went mad. When the rain came, he was ready.

Seven churches joined together one summer for youth camp. On the last evening, the senior pastor of each church was asked to tell his story of conversion and faith.

There were some real tearjerkers—former lives of crime, dirt, and mayhem turned into glory by God's grace.

Then Homer Hanna got up. Homer is now director of an orphanage. Kids are drawn to him.

"I don't have much to tell," he began. "I decided God wanted me to be a minister when I was twelve years old. I realized that in order to fulfill that calling, it would be best to keep my life real simple.

"I started going with Marilyn, my wife-to-be, when we were thirteen. The first time we kissed, I got weak all over. It wasn't long till we were touching tongues and breathing real hard and holding each other closer and closer."

The kids were listening now. "Then came the big decision," he continued. "Would we go all the way? We decided to keep it simple. We almost died waiting for our wedding night and we almost killed ourselves on our wedding night!

"In high school they had chug-a-lug contests. The idea was to see which guy could gulp down the most beer the fastest. The guy who was the last to throw up or pass out was the winner.

"I figured I could wait to be a winner at something else. So I don't have much of a story. I just try to keep it simple."

Homer hardly had a moment to himself after that. There was

always a kid who needed to talk with him. With youngsters, he's a miracle worker, miraculous changes happen to the children who hang out with Homer. That's because he lives in miracle territory—where you perform before the storm.

GO BEFORE YOU KNOW

Abraham is the second example of putting oneself in miracle territory. As you know, he is considered the "Father of Faith." Whenever someone wants to illustrate faith, they talk about Abraham.

The one constant that runs through Abraham's relationship with God was his going-not-knowing mentality. When God said go, Abraham didn't ask for a road map. He simply pulled up stakes and took off. "It was faith that made Abraham obey when God called him to go to a strange land. He left without knowing where he was going" (Hebrews 11:8).

You're in miracle territory when you go before you know.

"Blessing is the inward
cessation of wanting."

Does this sound like God only blesses the foolhardy? Do you have to be crazy to be a Christian? Isn't this a bit Jim Jonesy? Not at all. Those people didn't follow God to Guyana. They followed Jim Jones. "Yes, but they *thought* they were following God! How do you know when it's God who's talking?" The only answer I have is, "Look at the blessing." What did Abraham experience as a result of his go-before-you-know? He experienced blessing. And what is that? Wealth? Power? Good health?

Nope. *Blessing* is the inward cessation of wanting. It's the knowledge that "*It's okay*"—okay to be who I am, what I am.

It's knowing I have a purpose. In a word, *blessing* is grace. It is hearing God say, "You are my beloved child in whom I take great delight!" God's promise to Abraham was first and foremost, "I will *bless* you."

The way to know *things* is to gather all of the information on the subject and then make a commitment based upon the data. Knowledge comes before commitment.

The way to know persons is exactly the opposite. Commitment comes before knowledge.

Lois and I dated for five years before we married. From the time she was thirteen and I was fifteen, we spent more time and shared more secrets with each other than with anyone else. But after we married, we were amazed to discover that we neither knew each other nor really loved each other. Our previous relationship had been built on everything except a lifetime commitment. *We had to commit before we could know and love.*

Perhaps this is why people who live together before they marry are more apt to divorce than those who don't, because their relationship is built on everything except "till death do us part." They live together without the one indispensable ingredient of knowing and loving—"forsaking all others and cleaving only unto."

Abraham suffered. You know the story. First he became an alien in a strange land. He traded in stability for a tent. Then after finally having the son he always yearned for, he was asked by God to give him up. "Take your son," God said, "your only son.... Offer him as a sacrifice to me" (Genesis 22:2).

And Abraham saddled up. When his son asked after the ram for the sacrifice, Abraham could reply, "God himself will provide one" (Genesis 22:8). Hebrews 11:15 says Abraham did not think about what he'd left behind. If he had, he would have returned.

I was hunting in Eastern Alberta in the winter. It was ten degrees below zero, and there was snow and ice everywhere. We had to hunt from the truck to keep from freezing to death. On the first morning, I was so keyed up. We gobbled breakfast and jumped into the truck just before daybreak.

All of the forward gears were busted. Only reverse worked. "What are we going to do?" I asked the guide.

"We'll have to back up to the nearest town and get another vehicle."

"How far is that?"

" 'Bout forty miles."

Off we went, backing down the narrow-gauge road with huge snowbanks on each side. We started out at around twenty miles per hour, I'd guess. The odometer doesn't work in reverse.

As the guide's neck stiffened up, he sped up to thirty miles per hour, then forty, then to terror speed.

Things were going surprisingly well, considering the ice and all, until we came up behind this farmer pulling a trailer full of heifers. He was going about ten miles per hour and had no rearview mirrors. We followed him a long time. Finally there was an open straight stretch. The guide inched out into the oncoming lane and gunned it.

The Ukrainian farmer had no idea anyone was within miles of him, until he glanced over at us. We could almost touch him! His eyes were wide with terror. Later he told us that he thought his truck had stopped, and he didn't know it. Then he thought we were meeting him, and he hadn't seen us. Anyway, he plowed into the snowbank, the trailer came loose, and heifers went everywhere.

We stopped and took time to determine that everyone was okay and then took off. As we rounded the last curve leading into town, the road was a mass of flashing red lights, squad cars with Royal Canadian Mounted Police written on the side.

"Spread 'em. Hands over your head." The Mountie looked at my driver's license, then at the rifle in the truck. "Texas," he growled in disgust.

"Look," I said, "I'm sorry about the farmer. We meant no harm. I'll pay for the damages. Besides, I really cannot think of one single thing we did wrong."

"Oh, yes, you did!" he shot back. "We have a law in Canada," he bellowed. "You can't go forward—backward!" I paid a total of $1,327 to learn you can't go forward backward in Canada.

I've paid a lot more to learn the same is true in my life with God. How much of our lives do we spend trying to go forward while looking into the past—old regrets, resentments, hurts, hatreds, and guilt? No wonder the miraculous is so rare. You're in miracle territory when you go before you know and when you don't try to go forward backward.

EYES ON THE PRIZE

The writer to the Hebrews uses Moses as another example of how to put ourselves in miracle territory (Hebrews 11:24-28). You know the Moses story: Born a Hebrew and raised as a prince in Pharaoh's palace while his fellow Hebrews suffered in slavery, Moses never lost his social conscience.

By the time he reached adulthood, he had a messiah complex. He could right the wrongs of oppression by violent means, but to his dismay, the Hebrews didn't want to be liberated. So when Moses took up the sword, he found himself alone.

Moses fled to the desert, became a sheepherder, and forsook his dream. The story goes that one day he saw a bush aglow in the desert, not an uncommon occurrence according to some scholars. The Scripture says, "When God saw that Moses was coming closer, he called to him" (Exodus 3:4). Moses never lost his capacity to wonder.

Moses' capacity to dream, to leave ruts, enabled him to move into miracle territory. But where does this capacity come from? Have you ever wondered why some people never lose the courage to try again while others never muster enough courage to try the first time?

Hebrews 11:26 gives the answer: "He reckoned that to suffer scorn for the Messiah was worth more than the treasures of Egypt, *for he kept his eyes on the future reward"* (italics mine).

He kept his eyes on the prize! People stand up well under pressure when they keep their eyes on the prize. They die well and they lose well. One of my favorite lines is from the poem, "The Quitter," by Robert Service.

> It's easy to cry that you're beaten and die.
> It's easy to crawfish and crawl.
> But to fight and to fight when hope's out of sight,
> Why, that's the best game of all.
> And though you come out of each grueling bout
> All broken and beaten and scarred,
> Just have one more try, it's dead easy to die.
> It's the keeping on living that's hard.[3]

Do you remember the haunting words of Martin Luther King on the eve of his death? He acknowledged that there had been threats against his life. "But I have been to the edge of the Promised Land," he said. "And I'm not fearin' any man."

In 1965, I was still in school, commuting back and forth five hundred miles three times a week. I was a junior minister at a large church in Houston. Occasionally, the senior pastor would let me preach.

As fortune would have it, a search committee from a newly founded church near the Manned Spacecraft Center came to hear the senior pastor on a Sunday when I was speaking.

Monday I answered the phone. The voice on the other end said, "I'm from the new church near NASA, and I want to talk to you about coming to be our pastor."

They came and drove me around the beautiful new neighborhoods surrounding NASA. We toured the Center. I even got to fly the Lunar Excursion Module training craft.

I met John Glenn and Gus Grissom and Ed White who would later become a good friend. Next we toured the lovely new church plant. "We filled it the first Sunday," my host said, "and we're ready to build again."

Then they took me to see the parsonage. It was unbelievable! After we'd walked through it, the chairman of the committee said, "We've prayed about this matter, and we believe you're the man."

"That's how I had it figured, too," I said.

"Now, about your doctoral work," he said. "We don't want a par- time pastor. This job is for a professional. You'll have to forego that and settle for your master's degree."

I said I would, but I regretted saying it immediately. I was troubled and couldn't rest. I had six years of study and depriving my family invested, and I could see the end of the tunnel.

When I returned to the seminary, I went to see Dr. T. B. Maston. He had a son my age who was autistic and bedridden. He and Mrs. Maston had not left the boy unattended by one of the two of them for thirty years.

I told him my story. He rested his chin on his two thumbs and listened without expression. When I had finished, he said, "Hebrews 11:26, and there's the door."

That was it. He turned his attention to his desk, and I walked out. I went to my cubicle in the graduate studies section and read Hebrews 11:26. "[Moses] reckoned that to suffer scorn for the Messiah was worth more...for he kept his eyes on the future reward."

Four years passed before I became Doctor Mann. Twenty-six years later I had the chance to found and grow a "dream church."

I was in the NASA area a few months back to do a wedding. I drove by that "dream church" in that "dream neighbor-hood"—lots of weeds and cracking paint. As my son and I sat in the car looking at the little church, he said, "Papa, I'm sure glad you're into burning bushes instead of roses."

We laughed. Then he said, "You think you'll ever stop to smell the roses?"

"Yep. When I die I want you to put a spray of roses on my casket. When the undertaker closes it, you can say, 'Well, Papa finally stopped to smell the roses.'"

FIGHT THE FIGHT

The Egyptian army led by an angry Pharaoh was at their back. The Red Sea was before them. You've seen the movie; the Israelites marched toward the sea. They made a decision to "fight the fright." You're in miracle territory when you march straight into the sea of fear, when you decide to defy it.

Not a day goes by that we're not challenged by fear: fear of failure, fear of retribution, fear of losing space, face, and place.

There's a saying: "Do the thing you fear and the death of fear is certain." One of the most successful treatments for phobias is getting people to do the one thing they most fear. Claustrophobics lock themselves in tight places. People who are afraid of heights are left in the tops of trees. Most come out just fine.

Many fears tyrannize us that we are unaware of on the con-scious level. I'm thinking of John, for example. He had a lovely wife, two towheaded boys, and a profitable business. But he was an absolute jerk when it came to relationships. He gave more money to the church than anyone. Actually, com-pared to what he was making, he was giving only the sleeves of his vest.

He wanted to run things, and he had for years. I hadn't been there long before he tried to run me. On election day, my wife had been seen voting in her bathing suit with "only the skimpiest of cover-ups on." He would have me to know that the Bible said ministers should manage their wives in upright and moral ways and that this had better not happen again.

I invited him to step into my office where I closed and locked the door. "John," I said, "how did you become such an unhappy person?" He bristled. "I'll not take that from you! Who do you think you are, Sigmund Freud?"

"Yes, you will take this from me," I said quietly, "or you'll take a good whipping. I don't allow people to question my wife's character. I know it isn't Christian, but I'd rather go to hell for breaking your nose than let you bully me."

He tried to get me fired and couldn't. So he quit coming to church. About a month later, I walked into his office and shut the door.

> *"You're in miracle territory when you march straight into the sea of fear, when you decide to defy it."*

"I want you to come back to church," I said. "And I also want to know the answer to the question I asked you. How did you become so unhappy?" I didn't tell him that his wife had been to see me. She was about to leave him because of his verbal abuse of her and the boys.

Somehow, I struck a chord deep inside him. Out of the blue, he blurted, "You know my mother died when I was six."

"No, I didn't," I lied.

"On the day of her funeral my father sat the three of us boys down and said, 'We're all going to act like men at the service. We shall not soil your mother's image by showing grief. Mom was a Christian. She wouldn't want us grieving like pagans.'"

He was not crying as he continued. He was quietly bitter. "I broke down at the funeral," he said. "When we got home, my father scolded me in front of the others for dishonoring my mother. I made a vow, Preacher," he hissed, "that I would never let anyone hear me cry again."

This man was afraid. He was afraid to cry, afraid to say, "I love you," afraid to be close to anyone. And he hated God whom he had obviously identified with his father. This accounted for his rancor toward the church and its pastors and also for his abuse of his wife and his anger at mine.

"I'll make you a deal," I told him. "I'll fight the fight if you'll fight the *fright*." "Huh?" he said. "I vow to be your friend if you vow to begin this moment to defy the demons in your soul. Your sick daddy is *not* your heavenly Father. That's the place to start. Then you do the things you fear the most. Seek help. Say 'I love you.' Refuse to bully people. Spend some time with your boys. And learn to cry."

I never saw him again. No miracles happened. Why? Miracles happen only in miracle territory. And where is that? Well, you will know you're there when you perform before the storm, go before you know, keep your eyes on the prize, and fight the fright.

6

The Steam of Self-Esteem

One Sunday evening I received a call on my live talk TV program. Joann of Texas (not her real name) wanted to know if the Bible expressly forbade suicide. Could I give her chapter and verse?

I said, "No, but the Bible sees all of life as being on loan from God. It is not ours to take. To take your own life is the same as taking some one else's."

"Then suicide is a sin against God. Right?" she said.

"Look," I said. "Do we need to talk, Joann?"

"What do you mean?"

"I mean I want to know about your interest in suicide. Why the question?"

"Oh, I was just wondering," she said. "Bye."

This morning I received a letter from her, which was written ten days ago. It has only just reached me because I am in retreat writing this book. She starts by saying, "I don't agree that taking your own life is the same as taking another's life, because if you take another's life, that person has no choice whether to live or die. But if you take your own life, it's by choice."

Then she proceeded to tell me her story. Her mom died

when she was nine months old, leaving her dad with six children to raise. Her aunt and uncle took in all of the kids and raised them. "We never attended church," she said, "but as you often say on your show, when it came to helping and loving others, our home was a church."

She went on to say that she had married a construction worker and lived in twenty-one different states, never had children, and was widowed in mid-life. She sold her mobile home and moved to a small town where she knew no one. Let her tell the rest.

> Most of my family are gone now. I have two sisters left from my immediate family. I haven't seen the oldest for thirty-five years.
>
> You were right in your feeling when you asked, "Do we need to talk?" but I refused because no amount of talking can change my circumstances.
>
> I was fine until 1986 when I obtained several credit cards. They just came in the mail. I guess it was because I had always paid my bills and had a good credit rating.
>
> I don't know what happened, Dr. Mann. I never bought furnishings or took lavish trips or bought clothes. Mostly I got cash advances. Then I used other cards to get cash to pay the cash advances. Things just snowballed.
>
> Two years ago I ran out of cards to charge against other cards. My savings were gone and my $700 Social Security would not begin to address my problem... The finance charges, late payment charges, over-the-limit charges, and 18-20 percent interest charges have run the payoff up to $40,000.
>
> My circumstances are caused by my own stupidity. I have no one but myself to blame. I have always had such a good life and then to foul it up in so short a time and not even quite know how I did it!

There's no way out for me. The creditors hound me day and night.

On TV, I heard you talk about a man who climbed to the upper deck of Yankee Stadium and jumped off. He left a note saying he was no more than a peanut in Yankee Stadium and had decided to squash himself;

I feel the same way. For three months I've been making plans. I've given my personal things to a relative. I have my personal papers in order, and yet I will leave such a mess behind.

Please do not judge me harshly for what I am doing and remember me in your prayers.

> God Bless You,
> Joann of Texas

I am trying to contact Joann now. I don't know if she's still alive. I fear she is not. But I do know we don't have to be suicidal to feel the self-hatred she feels.

There have been countless books, seminars, and speeches on self-esteem. We have been inundated by commentary on the subject. Yet, "feeling like a peanut in Yankee Stadium" continues to be the number one killer of the human spirit.

**"*Feeling like a peanut in Yankee Stadium'*
continues to be the number one killer of the
human spirit."

Of all of the things Joann says in her letter, three sentences say the most: (1) "My circumstances are caused by my own stupidity." (2) "I have no one to blame but myself." (3) "There's no way out for me."

I can see many other things in her letter. I pray to God there's still time to point them out to her.

For example, why did she "lose it" with the credit cards? Early trauma (Mom died)? Nomadic uprooted life (no children, lived in twenty-one different states)? Widowed? Moved to a strange place? Family all gone now except for sisters she hasn't seen?

I hope I get to tell her that spending sprees are quite often grief reactions. I hope I get to tell her that she may have decided to declare war on herself because she felt guilty or angry over the deaths of everyone she was ever close to.

I failed to mention the part of her letter where she says she never cries. Oh, yes, she does! I see a lot of weeping going on in her credit card mania.

There's no use in telling her that forty thousand dollars isn't the end of the world. She'd never hear it because she looks at herself and sees nothing but a big zero.

Nothing kills the human spirit like low self-esteem. And the opposite is also true. Nothing drives the engine of human achievement and goodness like high self-esteem. "There's no steam like self-esteem!"

Here's a question for you. Give me the first answer that comes into your mind. Don't think about it. Just react to it.

If you could be anyone in the world, living or dead, who would you want to be?

Was your answer, "Me!"? If you'd rather be you than anyone else, you're cooking with the steam of self-esteem. If you answered someone else, you're in the vast majority along with me! I have rarely ever wanted to be me. I've spent most of my life wanting to be someone and somewhere else.

The secret to Jesus' power was not His ability to perform dazzling wonders, but His self-esteem. The dazzling wonders, in fact, had two negative effects. They made the establishment hostile, and they whetted the public's appetite for more wonders.

The steam of Jesus' profound effect on the world was that He never wanted to be anyone else but Himself.

Please read the third and fourth chapters of Matthew's gospel with this thought in mind. They are really not so much about Jesus' baptism and temptation as they are about the power of self-esteem.

Jesus begins His public ministry by submitting Himself to baptism. He declares publicly that He knows what He is to do with His life and is willing to do it.

Immediately after accepting His life-purpose, a dove descends and lights on His shoulder. Then the voice of God states: "Behold, this is My beloved Son, in whom I am well pleased" (Matthew 3:17, NKJV). Or loosely translated, "This is the Son I love! Every time I look at Him, I want to sing the doxology!" So Jesus lets God tell Him who He is. Then it says, "The Spirit of God [symbolized by the dove] led Him into the wilderness to be tempted by the devil" (Matthew 4:1).

The three temptations which Jesus had to face are really the three big lies about self-esteem which we all have to face. The devil is the creator of the lie. Here's the point: Immediately after Jesus is told who He is, His self-image comes under attack by three big lies which are designed to destroy that self-image. It is no different with us. These are *our* temptations as well.

WITHOUT BREAD, YOU'RE DEAD

Is it a coincidence that our most popular nickname for money is bread? "The devil said to Jesus, 'If You are God's Son, You gotta make bread!'" (Matthew 4:3, author's translation).

The first temptation of Jesus was not about accumulating followers by filling their bellies but the temptation to identify Himself by the amount of "bread" He could make. "Let what You have tell You who You are," said the devil. Jesus was being invited to judge His self-worth by His material worth, to buy into the myth that says, "Without bread, you're dead."

Some years back, Myron Madden wrote a book entitled *The Power to Bless.* Recently John Trent and Gary Smalley revived the central idea of Madden's book in a similar book called *The Blessing.*[1]

Madden says that every child is cursed and blessed early in life. The curse comes from being little in a big world (powerless) and from internalizing every negative experience.[2] That is, whenever something goes wrong, the child blames himself for it.

And he makes vows, says Madden. If his parents fight, he vows that when he gets big and has power, he will fix all of the conflicts in the world. If he hears his parents fretting over the lack of money, he vows that when he gets big, he will make enough money to calm the fears of all whom he loves.

The result is that many children in America grow up having vowed to make more money than any normal person could earn in three lifetimes.

It's important to remember that when we grow up, we forget these childhood vows on the conscious level. But the child always remains buried down there on the unconscious level where we feel.

The child within drives us more than we know. How can you identify childish vows buried within you? By looking at those areas of your life where you make unrealistic demands on yourself.

In which segments of your life are you trying to exceed your limits? Are you a mom who believes she can actually keep the house spotless with three kids in it? Are you a person who readily surrenders your rights and dignity for the sake of harmony? Or is it the opposite—you fight over the smallest infringement or offense? Are you trying to fix people you cannot fix? Are you trying to buy more than you can afford?

Where are your expectations unrealistic? There dwells the child, who in his feeling of powerlessness, vowed that someday he would get even, get ahead, and fix everything.

Nowhere does the child within show himself more in American society than in the getting, keeping, and consuming of "bread." We *are* our stuff.

Why do we buy a thirty thousand dollar car when a ten thousand dollar one will perform the same practical function? Because the thirty thousand dollar car tells us we are in the thirty thousand dollar class of human beings.

I have noticed that many ministers, myself included, define themselves in more materialistic terms than they would like to admit. For years I tended to judge my worth in terms of how much money I could raise. Boy, was I in for some self-hatred! I was pastoring fellow American materialists who judged their self-worth in terms of "bread" as well. So I was judging myself by how much they gave, and they were judging themselves by how much they could keep. And I wondered why they seemed so angry every time I talked about stewardship! One of my closest friends even said to me, "You know, when you get off of the subject of grace and onto the subject of money, you start growing fangs and wolf hair. You're no longer Dr. Jekyll. You're Mr. Hyde."

I felt liberated when I finally told them: "I am no longer what you give to God. If you choose to be what you keep from Him, that's entirely between you and Him." They haven't been so surly since then. In fact, they're becoming more generous all the time.

There's no steam like self-esteem for separating who we are from what we have. Jesus showed this to Satan when He answered the lie. "The Scripture says, 'Man cannot live on bread alone, but needs every word that God speaks'" (Matthew 4:4).

We need *the word God speaks to us* if we're going to resist the lie! And what word is that? "This is the child I love! Every time I look at him/her I want to sing the doxology!"

We were made for relationships with persons, not things. We were made to be spoken to by a loving Father who wants to sing the doxology every time He looks at us. But if we have not heard His words—within, where the child lives—we shall choose stuff.

Paul Tillich used to talk about "Thingification"—the condition of the person who touches things to see if he is real, not to see if the things are.

In our church family, I can name fourteen millionaires who went broke between 1985 and 1991. Since the Arabs opened the oil spigot and the regulators shut off the credit line, there has been a bloodbath in Texas. I never realized that going broke is a grief experience. For every one of my friends, it was not just the money they had lost. It was a whole way of life, including the entire mystique that goes with the Horatio Alger myth.

These men and women had worked hard and taken huge risks and given generously and dealt honestly. There wasn't an Ebenezer Scrooge in the bunch. But try as they had, they could not separate who they were from what they had and did. I know. Because, you see, I was one of them.

I don't mean to sound condescending, but most preachers who speak eloquently about money haven't had much of it. How do I know? Because they speak too flippantly to have had it and used it wisely and lost it.

Anyway, I am happy to report that all of the "Former Fourteen"—that's how we refer to ourselves have fared well. We smell things we never smelled before and enjoy what we never enjoyed. And laugh a healing kind of laughter we never laughed.

Most and best, we have learned the hard way that "man does not live by bread." My wife puts it this way: "Money can't buy happy. It only allows you to take happy to a lot more places."

We have learned that we are not what we have, and we think the lesson was worth the money. (Of course, now that we've learned the lesson, we'd like to have the money back!) However, we don't have to have it in order to be and to like who we are. There's no steam like the steam which drives us beyond the lie which says, "Without bread, you're dead."

WITHOUT FAME, YOU'RE LAME

The second temptation thrown at Jesus was to jump from the tallest tower of the temple in Jerusalem and be rescued by God's angels. "If You are God's Son, throw Yourself down, for the Scripture says, 'God will give orders...not even Your feet will be hurt'" (Matthew 4:5-6).

"If you can't be rich, then be famous." Isn't this the great American motto? For those who cannot be what they *have*, there is always the opportunity to be what they *do*.

Satan is saying to Jesus, "Okay, if you're not going to buy into the big lie about 'stuff,' let me offer the one about 'stunts.' Be a sensation! Do something truly extraordinary with your life. Don't worry about getting hurt. Look at it this way. Without fame, you're lame anyway."

Robert Schuller is right. Most of us are not who we think we are or who others think we are. We are who we think others think we are. And what we want to hear is that we are legends in our own time. "Just spell my name right" is more important than "Tell the truth about me." From the first moment, a well-meaning parent or teacher tells us to go out and "be somebody," and we get the message: "Right now you are nobody."

"I'm gonna live forever. They're gonna know my name." That's the beginning line of the theme song of a Broadway hit called *Fame*. The devil said, without it, you're lame. If you can't be what you have, be what you do.

Ministers are not immune to this second lie either. Here's a personal example. I have had many a meal and golf game with Willie Nelson, but never without having someone interrupt us when they recognized him. Willie is always gracious. I've seen several dinners get cold because he couldn't get to them.

We were having lunch one day when a lady rushed up to the table. But this time she not only grabbed Willie, she also grabbed me! "I watch you on TV every week!" she said. "You're simply wonderful."

After she left, I said to Willie, "God help me, I loved it. Do you ever grow tired of it?"

"Naw!" he said. "You just learn to pretend that it bothers you. Heck, isn't this what we all used to lie awake nights dreaming about!"

The way to see through the lie that says, "Without fame, you're lame," is Jesus' way. Listen to His answer to Satan's second offer. "The Scripture says, 'Don't put the Lord your God to the test'" (Matthew 4:7). This is His way of saying, "God has His own scheme for My life, and He has set that scheme within a world which operates according to certain laws. *Thou shall not push the limits of God's scheme!"*

To know "your scheme" and to know that you are a person of worth when you follow it is the only way to separate who you are from who "they" say you are.

It is entirely okay to be rich and famous, by the way, if it's God's scheme for you. There is the proper having and the proper doing. And no one but God can identify your scheme. But if your scheme is His scheme, you can hear Him saying, "Look at my beloved child in whom I take great delight." There's no steam like self-esteem for facing the big lie which says "without fame, you're lame."

WITHOUT CLOUT, YOU'RE OUT

The third big lie about self-worth has to do with rank or clout. We tend to determine our self-worth by who we're better than, smarter than, healthier than, whiter than, etc. Some religious folks have a love affair with being "righter than" everyone else.

Often we hear the phrase, "I'm bad, but I'm not as bad as..." This statement is no different from the Pharisee's "How glad I am that I am better than that tax collector over there" (Luke 18).

"What we want to hear is that we are legends in our own time."

Have you noticed how much our society is into the "We're Number One!" madness? From PeeWee League to the pros, we shout it. Well, I'd like to start a "We're Number Nothin'!" movement. It wouldn't get very far, but it could at least serve as a countermeasure to the lie which says, "Without clout, you're out."

The temptation to let who we're better than tell us who we are was Satan's third run at Jesus. He showed Jesus a vision of "all of the kingdoms" and said, "You will be king if You will worship me." It was an appeal to clout, to rank: "I am who I'm stronger than."

Jesus' answer was His final declaration of self-esteem. In essence, He says, "Let God be God" (Matthew 4:10). It was His way of saying, "I'm glad to be who I am. I am not My rank. God's number one while I'm on this earth fulfilling My mission."

So we live or die according to our self-esteem. Jesus' profound power stemmed from His absolute acceptance and delight with how God had made Him. He didn't want to be anyone else. Through the veil of the three big lies: (1) without bread, you're dead; (2) without fame, you're lame; (3) without clout, you're out—Jesus heard the voice of the Father saying, "This is the Son I love. Every time I look at Him, I want to sing the doxology!"

The question for us is: How do we hear the voice of the Father above the roar of the lies?

There are some simple clues in the passage we've been using. Reread Matthew 4:1-11. First, Jesus quit listening to the *liars*. Who are they? They are that collective reflection of us which are often called the media.

The media are nothing more than our projected tastes and values trying to sell and tell us what we want to buy and hear. If we don't buy the lie, they won't sell it. The media are most often simply our magnified and projected self-image.

I think "the Spirit of the age" in Scripture refers to the media. There is always a spirit of the age, a prevailing opinion about what's real and true and of value. A society gets into trouble when it cannot tell the real from the unreal. Then the liars have their way.

For example, in the 1960s, the "spirit of the age" told us to sever ties with all traditional commitments and to "go out and find ourselves." Millions of Americans left marriages and jobs and the restraints caused by their traditional ethics. Phrases like "Do your own thing" and "Pulling your own strings" became the mottos of the day.

The media—movies, print, news—fell into line and glamorized the "spirit," then sold it to us *en masse.*

By 1980, the folks who went looking for self found it—the self they had left behind when they went looking! So we had a resurgence of the "traditional values" of acquisition and easy credit, "go now and pay later." By 1990, a pervasive emptiness of the soul shadows the land.

One of the four megatrends of the nineties is said to be "The Respiritualization of Society." I would not be at all surprised to see Madison Avenue, the advertising capital of the world, selling "stuff" in the name of spiritual reformation.

To shut our ears to the liars simply means to refuse to listen to our own projected false values.

Other liars we must ignore are the innocent parent figures who had the curses passed on to them and are now passing them on unwittingly to us. Until we hear the Father's voice telling us who we are, we can only pass on what we've been given.

For instance, my son told me just the other day, "I wish you hadn't named me Gerald Mann II. I want my own name." He didn't say this in a petulant or rebellious way at all. He said it matter-of-factly. And he was right. Nothing brands a boy with his father's desire for cloned immortality more than being named "Junior" or "II." Remember, he was the unexpected son of my old age. I realize now that I wanted a "chip off the old block," and he was the only chip left.

> *"Jesus knew who He was, so He had no problem taking up the towel or the Cross."*

Jesus refused to listen to the liars. He also memorized the words of His real Father. It is more than preacher prattle to tell you that the Scriptures comprise the best lie-detector machine in the world. Jesus didn't wander into the desert unarmed. He knew the Father's Word. Every time Satan threw a lie at Him, He answered it with a truth from God. And when Satan threw a lie at Him garbed in a Scripture ("The Scripture says . . . your feet won't even be bruised"), Jesus answered him with another Scripture. The Father's voice is contained in what He has said in the past and in what He says now.

Finally, Jesus was able to hear the Father's voice because "the angels came" (Matthew 4:11). I believe angels are any and everyone God sends our way to love us unconditionally.

My grandmother was an "angel." She gave me the gift of delight. My sixth grade teacher, who was the first to tell me I could use words as a power for good, was an angel. Every church I've served has had "angels" who loved me because, rather than *if*.

Mrs. Robinson was my ninth grade algebra teacher. I was in trouble at school and failing. One day, she ordered me to stay after class. She never smiled, and we were all terrified of her. She delighted in flunking athletes, which was my only claim to fame.

After class, she closed the door. "I did a dumb thing last Friday night," she said. "I went to a stupid football game. Crazy parents yelling their heads off. Little girls in their budding nudities, prancing and screaming. Boys trying to knock each other senseless." She sighed. "But it wasn't all a waste. I discovered something. Anyone who is bright enough to dodge as many people on a football field as you can is certainly smart enough to pass Algebra I."

She swore me to a secret pact. If I would come to her home for two hours every Saturday, she would tutor me. I did and I passed.

Years later when I received my doctorate, I wrote her a note of thanks. Sometime later I received a reply:

> Dear Jerry,
>
> It was with great surprise that I learned you are now *Doctor* Mann! I was not surprised that you *could* do it but that you *would* do it.
>
> I am now past eighty, living alone in a one-room apartment with my cats and books. I am like the last leaf of autumn, hanging on as winter approaches.
>
> I taught school for over fifty years and yours is the first note of thanks that I have ever received.
>
> It came on a rainy day and cheered me as nothing has in years.

"Jesus said, 'Go away, Satan!' After that, the angels came" (Matthew 4:11).

The Father sees you, and He delights in what He sees. You

can believe that or you can believe the liars. You can let Him tell you who you are, or you can let "them" tell you.

How to keep hearing the Father? Ignore the liars! Live on the Word. Receive the angels.

Self-esteem—letting the Father tell me who I am—has everything to do with making the bad times over for good. That same Jesus who stood up to the three big lies of self-hatred also had to hear the Father's voice while immersed in suffering: while His own disciples failed to understand His message; while the religious community who should have welcomed Him was trying to kill Him; while His mother and brothers came to get Him because He seemed to have lost His marbles; and, yes, while He endured the Cross.

No doubt you have read and heard of the Last Supper as many times as I have. But I recently noticed something in John's version that I had missed previously. It speaks volumes to the way Jesus' self-esteem enabled Him to transform the trouble of the Cross into the triumph of the Resurrection.

Remember that His disciples still didn't understand that He had to die. They were simply enjoying the Passover Feast.

John says, after Judas had gone to tell the authorities where they could find and arrest Jesus, that "Jesus knew that the Father had given Him complete power" (John 13:3). "Complete power" means *finished power,* all the power He needed to see Him through the ordeal.

And what was the source of this power? The same old voice He had heard at the beginning three years earlier: "This is the Son I love, in whom I take great delight!" He was still letting God tell Him who He was!

Then John says, "Jesus knew that he had come from God and was going to God. So he rose from the table...and began to wash the disciples' feet" (John 13:3-5). When you know you've come from the Father and are going to the Father, you have no problem washing feet on the night before you die.

What a portrait of self-esteem! He knew who He was, so He had no problem taking up the towel or the Cross. The steam of self-esteem is our Father's voice. Can you hear it?

7

Every
Mountain
Is a Foothill

Y ears ago I attended the great Riverside Church in New York City where Ernest Campbell was the pastor. As I sat in that awesome place built and endowed by the Rockefellers, I was overwhelmed. Campbell's eloquent message was, "Nothing Stays Won." He quoted the Apostle Paul from 1 Corinthians 9:27: "I harden my body with blows and bring it under complete control, to keep myself from being disqualified after calling others to the contest."

Nothing stays won. Every war ever fought was supposed to be the last one. Every sweeping social reform was supposed to be the cure-all. Every medical breakthrough was supposed to eradicate "the plague" forever.

On the personal level, every time I conquer one weakness, it either resurrects or opens the door to a dozen more.

This is particularly true when it comes to hanging on to our faith in the midst of trouble. I have contended throughout this book that human life is a soul-making process. We are all "Adam and Eve," born unfinished but in God's image, and with the choice of using our pain to "make our souls" into His likeness. In order for suffering to have any meaning, we must give it meaning by using it for the good.

In this chapter, we are going to focus on one of the harshest realities which accompanies this soul-making quest—*every mountain is a foothill.* Much of our suffering comes from the illusion that we can finish our soul-making and rest. The hard fact is that every time we climb a mountain of tribulation, we have not arrived at a stopping place. The mountain is only a foothill. We cannot lie back, rest, and look down on our achievements. We must look upward to the next mountain. Whoever wrote, "And they lived happily ever after," was simply trying to find a convenient ending for a fairy tale. There is no *living* happily ever after.

Do you remember the scene when Jesus was on the Cross and He cried out, "My God, My God, why have You forsaken Me?" (Matthew 27:46, NKJV)? The words, "My God, My God," in Hebrew sounded a lot like the word *Elijah,* the name of the Old Testament rescuer-prophet.

Jesus' followers who were standing near the cross still didn't believe He would die, so they jumped to conclusions. "He's calling for Elijah!" they began to shout. "So that's it! Everything's going to be all right! Elijah's coming! Elijah's coming!" But the text says, "Jesus again gave a loud cry, and breathed his last" (Matthew 27:50).

The hard message is one we never want to hear: *Elijah's not coming.* We don't climb the mountain and wait for Elijah to come take us home. We have to keep climbing. Every mountain is a foothill.

There is a common error that God's people have repeated in every era from biblical times until now. We are always confusing *tenancy* with *ownership.*

A tenant is a manager. He is given something by an owner to tend, nurture, and multiply. My grandfather was a sharecropper. The landowner let him use the land, and they shared the proceeds.

As the years passed, Grandfather was so good at farming that he became rather cavalier about the farm. He spoke more and more of "my farm." You know what happened. One day the owner took the place.

God's people—you and I—are tenants on this earth. Not even our lives are *ours.* We own nothing, which means that we cannot confuse mountains with foothills and live. There is no height we can attain and then sit back and survey all we have done and won. Jesus told a story about one farmer who tried that, the only person Jesus ever called a fool (Luke 12:13-21).

If we are going to transform trouble into triumph, we shall have to practice the every-mountain-is-a-foothill principle. I agree with Campbell that this principle was the secret to Paul's great life. He never rested upon his laurels. He never saw success as permanent.

There's an almost comical passage in his last prison letter to his young protégé, Timothy (2 Timothy 4:6-13). He starts out saying he knows his time is up. The hour of his execution is

---

> **"Every time I conquer one weakness,
> it either resurrects or opens the door
> to a dozen more."**

---

near. He says he is ready. He has no fears or regrets. He's actually looking forward to his death. Then in the next breath, he tells Timothy to bring Mark to help in the missionwork and not to forget his coat and his books! One minute he's all but dead. The next, he's planning to climb another mountain. *Every person should die while planning his next climb!*

Every mountain is a foothill when it comes to grieving. Many have spoken of the stages of grief which follow the aftermath of tragedy.

There is denial. We say, "This is a dream, a nightmare! It hasn't really happened." Then we start the bargaining. "If you'll make this go away, I'll do such and such." Then come the tears and wailing that are usually followed by a numbness. Just as parts of the body go numb when they are first traumatized, so does the soul.

Then the long, painful questioning sets in, accompanied by fits of guilt and anger and words like *what-if, if-only,* the dominant question is *why*.

Each of these stages is a towering mountain. But to rest upon any one of them is to wither within.

And the final stage of grief is really only a foothill, too. Acceptance of tragedy is the stage where I stop asking "why?" and start asking "what?" and "how?"—what to do with my life from this moment on and how to live with the given fact that tragedy has occurred. I shall never know the "why?" so *how* do I get on with it?

Let me share a few things that have worked for me when I have reached the "how" stage of grief, that is, when I have accepted the fact that tragedy has occurred and have made the choice to get on with it instead of remaining frozen.

WHAT FOR CHRIST—LATELY?

First, I have found that my past experiences with God are not enough for dealing with present hurts. Past-tense faith doesn't cure present-tense pain.

I should hurry to say that past-tense experiences do give me hope. Because God *was* there in the past, I believe He is here in the present. However, I need to *feel* His presence in the now.

The only way I am able to put myself in the place where God can soothe my pain now is to find someone who's hurting and try to help them. I know this sounds ridiculous if you're currently trying to transform a tragedy in your life. It may even sound cruel to tell someone who's just lost a loved one or has been pronounced terminally ill to turn their lives outward and help others.

Remember, I said this is for those who have already climbed the mountains of denial, bargaining, anger, guilt, and questioning. This is for the ones who are ready for the "how" mountain.

There's no better way to "get on with it" and feel God's presence than to help the hurting. That's what Father Henri Nouwen's great book, *The Wounded Healer,* is all about.

He cites a Jewish legend about a Rabbi who is looking for the Messiah and runs into Elijah. Elijah tells him the Messiah is outside the gates with the sick and wounded and dying. He is wounded, too. "How shall I recognize Him if He, too, is wounded?" asks the Rabbi. He is told that while the others bind and unbind their wounds all at once, the Messiah unbinds His one at a time, so that He can be ready to help the others if He's needed. He will not be bound or unbound in such a way as to prevent Him from helping the others.[1]

POINT: Every mountain is a foothill when it comes to grief. We are never finished climbing. And the first step up every mountain is to ask ourselves what we are doing to heal people for Christ in the present.

I have a preacher friend who has led a church for years in a large city where most of the population is black. Thirty years ago he was a leading force for racial justice in the city. His church used to be filled and emptied three times each Sunday morning. Thousands of people of all shapes and colors came to hear him.

I talked to him not long ago. He's now in his seventy-sixth year. The church now has about one hundred fifty in worship. "Everybody worships at their own risk," he said. "Our neighborhood is one of the crack cocaine capitals of America. I am now threatening the drug establishment the way I threatened

---
"Heal your hurt by healing hurts."
---

the racist establishment years ago. Many of our men must come to services armed.

"I imagine you'll be readin' about me in the obituary soon. Some fool will shoot me, or I'll die preaching or in bed. But I'll tell you this. When God comes for me, He's gonna catch me doin' somethin' for Him *lately!*"

Karl Menninger once told me that in all of the years of treating the emotionally battered, he never once saw a person who didn't get better when they turned their lives outward to help someone else.

Every mountain is a foothill when it comes to what you're doing for Christ lately. The cure for hurt is to heal other hurts.

I have a silver-plated tin cup on my desk that has a special meaning. Four years ago during the Christmas season, I received a letter from an inmate in state prison. The inmate had heard me speak years before. He had gotten into drugs, which meant a constant need for cash, which meant looking for cash illegally, which meant embezzlement.

He got probation, sobered up, and then made the biggest mistake of his life. As a result of his familiarity with the legal system, he started impersonating a lawyer! And he won several cases before they caught up to him!

Well, there was no probation this time; lawyering without a

license is a capital offense. He received ten years counting the time he received when his probation was revoked. Four of them were without parole.

The letter came at a time when my own boat was loaded. My father had died in the early fall. My mother was at death's door. We had our infant granddaughter because her parents were at war again. And, of course, Christmas is the season when the pastor must be jolly whether he wants to be or not.

My heart ached for the inmate. His family had rejected him. He wanted a letter and a friend. I jotted him a one-page note. I know it sounds pathetic, but it was the last drop I had to give.

On Christmas Sunday, I read Scott's haunting letter at church. There wasn't a dry eye in the place. All Scott wanted was to be remembered by someone who cared while he spent Christmas in a cold, uncaring place. Coincidentally, the Attorney General of Texas was in the service. My A.A. friends have a saying: "Coincidence is God's way of remaining anonymous." The Attorney General took Scott's prison number down on a church bulletin and later checked into his case personally.

Scott was released from prison and came to town. He was baptized in our church. We got him a job. He fell off of the wagon two or three times. My people just kept on loving him. He has now been straight for several years and has a good job. He married a lady in our church the week before I left to write this.

One day he came by to talk. "The letter you wrote me in prison saved my life," he said.

"It was only a one-page note, for God's sake!" I answered.

"Yes, I know," he said. "But when you have no letters, a one-pager is a feast."

He gave me the tin cup, silver-plated because he wanted the inscription to last. "I assure you that anyone who gives you a drink of water because you belong to me will certainly receive his reward" (Mark 9:41).

All I had left that Christmas was a cup of cold water. I was hurting so badly myself. But it was enough. Heal your hurt by healing hurts. "You will find Him among the wounded." "But how shall I recognize the Messiah?" "He will have His wounds bound up. But they will not be bound so tightly that He cannot bind up the wounds of the others."

WHO'S ON FIRST?

Every time I stand at the wedding altar with a young couple, I am reminded of the fragility of loyalty. As they say their vows and pledge the highest kind of commitment our language can muster, I know that many will not keep them.

Every mountain is a foothill when it comes to loyalty. Loyalties are never finished. Whoever invented the phrase "total commitment" should be placed on the same island with the "happily-ever-after" guy.

There's no such thing as *total* commitment. I lived for years thinking there was. It is the best sermon topic for an evangelist who is preaching to a church full of people who have already embraced the faith at least once. You can always get some of them to come forward at the end of the service by questioning their *total* commitment. Some even get baptized and rebaptized several times. The preacher asks, "Are you 100 percent committed to the will of God?" Obviously no one is. The ones who are honest enough to admit it make good "scores" for the evangelist.

Keith Miller helped me understand commitment in his book *The Becomers*.[2] He says commitment means "committing as much as you know about yourself to as much as you know about God." Obviously, commitment is a lifelong pursuit.

What does commitment have to do with transforming our

suffering? Simply this: The decision to use suffering for a higher good is a commitment, a leap of faith. It is like a man who does not know how to swim deciding to jump from a cliff into ten thousand fathoms of water.

We cannot transform trouble into triumph until we decide to trust God's promises that we *can*—until we decide "who's on first." And this commitment is never finished. About the time we think we have reached the pinnacle of loyalty to God in facing our woes, we discover that we haven't.

There is a moving story from the life of Martin Luther which illustrates how easily our commitment to God gets knocked off center. Luther is one of my favorites; he had a sense of humor and a sense of tolerance.

As you know, he was a devout Catholic priest who taught himself to read the Greek New Testament and in so doing realized that the Greek Bible related a different story from the Latin concerning how people are made right with God. Luther had his own "encounter with transcendence" one night in his barren little cell at the monastery. He was never the same again. Nor was the Western world.

After breaking with the Roman Church, establishing the Protestant German Church, marrying, and entering the golden years of his creativity, he was visited by tragedy. His beloved fourteen-year-old daughter Magdalena fell sick and was obviously dying.

At her bedside, Luther poured his heart out in prayer for her healing, but to no avail. Toward the end, he said to her: "Magdalena, my little girl, you would like to stay with your father here, and you would be glad to go to your Father in heaven?" "Yes, Father, as God wills," she said. Luther cursed himself because God had blessed him as no bishop had been blessed in a thousand years, and yet, "I cannot find it in my heart to praise and love You now."[3]

Luther discovered that every mountain is a foothill when it

comes to "who's on first?" in our lives. Loyalty to God is never finished. So do not be surprised when your trust is shaken. And do not be surprised to wake up someday to discover that your allegiances have become confused.

I read a news article the other day which said that in 1900 a survey was done among American parents. They were asked, out of the four professions—medicine, law, teaching, and ministry—which they would most want their children to pursue. The ministry was first, followed by teaching, medicine, and the law. According to the article, a recent survey was done asking parents the same question. Today's parents chose medicine first, then law, then teaching, with ministry running a distant last.[4]

I was indignant! No one wanted to do what I'm doing. I planned to singe the airwaves with a Sunday tirade on the subject. Then my son came in for our nightly visit. He gets up in my bed, and we talk. We've been doing this since he was small.

"I've been thinking about what God wants me to do with my life," he said. My heart froze in my chest. "Oh, God," I said under my breath, "don't let him be a minister!"

Your loyalties may not be what you think they are. Had I been responding to that survey, I would have chosen the same four in the same order!

What are your financial obligations? If someone were to invite you to do what you like to do most and at their expense, what commitments would prevent you from accepting?

There's a story recorded in Luke 9:57-62 that illustrates how easy it is to forget "who's on first." A man comes up to Jesus and says, "I will follow you wherever you go." Jesus chills the man's enthusiasm. "Foxes have holes, and birds have nests, but the Son of Man has no place to lie down and rest."

Then Jesus turns to a bystander and says, "Follow me."

He replies, "First let me go back and bury my father." Jesus chills him as well. "Let the dead bury their own dead. You go and proclaim the Kingdom of God."

Another bystander steps forward. "I will follow You, but let me go bid my family farewell." Again Jesus gives a hard reply. "Anyone who starts out to plow and keeps looking back is of no use for the kingdom of God."

Whatever you think of these exchanges between Jesus and His would-be followers, you can see that they illustrate how our seemingly legitimate commitments become excuses for non-commitment.

According to Matthew's version of the story (Matthew 8), the first guy was a rich ruler. He was pledging to forsake his purse and persona to follow Jesus. The second and third guys had reasonable requests— one to bury his father and the other to say good-bye to his family.

I think Jesus was using some real shock tactics to say that every mountain is a foothill when it comes to who's on first in your life. Commitment never gets finished. There will always be another mountain of trouble towering above the one you've just climbed. That's what soul making is all about—ingesting, digesting, and metabolizing our suffering.

WHERE GOD FINDS YOU

On the rare occasions when I have mustered the courage to heal my hurts by helping to heal others and when I have continued to reevaluate "who's on first," God has come to find me in some of the strangest places.

I went to a nursing home to visit the mom of a friend. "She's always prided herself in being an unbeliever," he said. "She told me on my high school graduation night that having me was the greatest disappointment of her life. I never saw my father. He was killed in the war. They married a week before he shipped out. She had many boyfriends. She never cried and never smiled."

She wanted to see a preacher. But not just any preacher, she wanted to see me. I seemed to have had a "troubled life" according to what she had heard from my sermons on TV. Maybe I could answer her one question.

She was sitting in a wheelchair. Her hands were gnarled and twisted from arthritis. "My question for you is this," she said. "Assuming there is a God, why would He leave me here on this miserable earth? I have no friends. I am estranged from my son. I can't even use the bathroom by myself. I would take my own life, but I'm too feeble even to do that!

"So what's your answer?" she demanded.

"My answer is that you sound like you could use a friend."

"Bullsh_ _!" she spat. "I need to know why I was born and why I've been so miserable and why I can't die!"

This went on for an hour. I would gently try to reach out to her, and she would resist. I tried to delve into her past. What about her mother and father? I used all of the usual nondirective techniques. Finally exhausted, I said, "The only reason I can think of for God's leaving you here is to show you that you aren't God and to show me I'm not either! I'm outta here!"

Off I went down the hall. As I hurried past a room, a little voice squeaked, "Dr. Mann?" I pretended not to hear it, but it tripped out of the door again, "Dr. Mann."

I went back. And there was another twisted, frail, arthritis-ravaged lady in a wheelchair. But her face was literally radiant. "Oh, I'm so glad you heard me!" she exclaimed. "They told me you might pass this way. You've been down there with Grump, haven't you? We all call her Grump. I think she's had gas all of her life, poor thing," she giggled.

She proceeded to recite to me the sermon I had preached on TV the previous Sunday. She was so full of life—no complaints, no endless clinical account of her physical ailments which were obviously many. She was an avid reader, everything from Homer to Tom Clancy. She smiled when she told me she was widowed after fifty-two wonderful years. No kids, she said.

I couldn't help comparing her with Grump down the hall. I had to ask her, "Do you ever wonder why God keeps you here on this earth?"

"Not for a minute!" she responded quickly. "I know why God's keeping me here. I told you I had no children, but that's not technically correct. I have a son. Somewhere. I haven't seen him for twenty years. Don't know where he is. He's had a hard life. I'm the only person in the world that's left to pray for him. God's keeping me here to pray for my boy."

Three years later the funeral director called and asked if I would do her funeral service. Only three people came. A man in his fifties, his wife in her early thirties, and a three-year-old girl. After the service, the man introduced himself. "I am her son," he said. "I'm glad I found her before it was too late for her to meet my wife and daughter." He pointed to the two standing at his side.

> *"The greater our attempts to heal and our courage to commit, the greater God's gracious support. 'Only when it's darkest do the stars come out.'"*

Every mountain is a foothill when it comes to being found by the Father. About the time you think you've seen all you're going to see of Him, you need to look up. *You ain't seen nothing yet!* When I fled Grump's room, exhausted and depressed, God could have been a million miles away. In fact, He was just two doors down the hall.

What I've been trying to say in all of this is that God finds us and "holds us up" in proportion to our daring to heal others and reevaluate our commitment to His way of doing life. The greater our attempts to heal and our courage to commit, the greater God's gracious support. "Only when it's darkest do the stars come out."

But the hard fact is that soul-making never gets finished. There will never be a day this side of heaven when we shall not have to choose whether to let our hurts defeat us or to use our hurts to help the hurting; whether to keep God on first or put ourselves there; whether to climb up to the next foothill where God can find us or live in the past where He used to be.

As for me, I believe in climbing. I believe that on top of the last mountain, I will be found by a God who still has some delightful surprises for me.

I love the play by Eugene O'Neill entitled *Lazarus Laughed*[5] about the man named Lazarus whom Jesus raised from the dead (John 11). In the play, Lazarus comes forth from the grave laughing, the spontaneous, unrestrained laughter of a person who knows something which no one else knows. It isn't long until Lazarus's friends get around to asking the big question. "What is it really like on the other side?" Lazarus simply laughs. "There is only laughter!" he says, "only the laughter of God!"

He goes on to tell them that we are all born out of the laughter of God and return to the laughter of God. "There is only laughter and only life!" he says.

Soon many people are coming to hear Lazarus. His laughter and joy are infectious. People begin to lose their fear and enjoy their freedom. As is typically the case, the religious authorities become threatened by such hilarity. Lazarus is scolded. He simply laughs. Finally he is threatened. If he does not stop his infernal laughing, they will kill him!

"Go ahead!" he welcomes. "There is only life. There is only laughter. The life and the laughter of God!"

Every mountain of trouble is a foothill for another mountain. But life is in the climbing while death is in the resting. I could not believe this if God did not come and find me in the midst of my "uphill world." And the God who finds me is always the God of life and laughter.

8

Winning
Is Beginning

Probably everyone who's a football fan knows what Green Bay Packer coach Vince Lombardi said about winning: "Winning isn't everything; it's the only thing." Critics of the competitive spirit have fired arrows at that remark, but I agree with it totally. The main purpose of football is to win. Darrell Royal, the legendary coach at the University of Texas, once did a filmed interview as a spoof for a banquet. The reporter asked him about the overemphasis placed on winning.

"I sure do agree with that!" said Royal. "You know, after I lost my first game at Texas, I read where Oliver Wendell Holmes said that losing builds character. Football is for team-work and discipline and motivating players to reach their personal best.

"I took heart from Mr. Holmes's remarks. Then we lost again, and I read some more of Mr. Holmes. He said life's greatest lessons come from losing and learning to live over it." Royal paused, deadpanned directly into the camera, and said, "Then we beat our archrival, Texas A&M. Afterward I thought a lot about everything I had learned. And I'd just like to say, 'Pi_ _ on Oliver Wendell Holmes!'"

I agree. I like to win at everything. I'm a competitive person. To dream the impossible dream and to reach for it brings out the best in us.

Consider this: Have you ever thought what life would be without death? What if there were no outer limit to your life? The whole point of a football game is to see what the players can achieve within a given time frame.

And so it is with our lives. We are *competing,* whether we like it or not. Life's meaning comes from trying to overcome the opponents that stand between us and our goals before the clock runs out. Take away the clock, and life would be boring at best.

Winning is important, not only in football but also in many other things. I agree with James Dobson when he says that we should help our children find something which they can "win at." So much of our self-esteem comes from being a winner at something.

My focus in this chapter is on winning as it relates to suffering. When can we say we are winning over our troubles? Does winning mean that there comes a time when the hurt is over? When I told my friend who had lost her three-year-old child that I was going to write a book about transforming trouble into triumph, she said, "Will you tell me what victory is? It's been ten years since our baby died, and it still hurts!"

In one of John Claypool's moving sermons which he delivered during his daughter's fatal struggle with leukemia, he defines victory over pain.[1] He uses the great passage from Isaiah 40:31 (NKJV) to describe the three kinds of victory that we can achieve over trouble. The verse reads: "But those who wait on the LORD shall renew their strength; they shall mount up with wings like eagles; they shall run and not be weary, they shall walk and not faint."

Sometimes we are able to "mount up with wings as eagles" in the face of trouble. The miraculous occurs. God delivers us. We soar in ecstasy. At other times, we receive an extra adrenaline burst or a positive energy which allows us to "run and not be weary," to work around and through our troubles with an uncanny strength.

These two types of victory over trouble are the ones most often described in the motivational, positive-thinking books. I believe in positive thinking. Negative thinking is a universal disease which stunts the human race.

But this chapter and this book are about the third kind of victory which Claypool points to in Isaiah's verse. *Sometimes you run out of possibilities!* Then what? All you can do is "Walk and not faint," or put one foot in front of the other.[2]

What I want you to see is that one-foot-in-front-of-the-other *is a method of winning!* It's not glamorous, but it's a victory. I like to put it this way: *In God's eyes, winning is beginning!* The premium is placed on the heart to start. He'll take the steps with you. The world loves winners; God loves beginners.

"If you're beginning to love God, neighbor, or self in the midst of the struggle, you're winning"

Jesus reduced religion to three fundamental relationships: loving God, loving neighbor, and loving self. He was relational, not doctrinal. While the religious community was arguing about proper beliefs, He talked about proper relationships. The last thing the world needed was another religion—more doctrine, more ritual, more law.

What the world did need, and still does, is to hear that all God requires is the "heart to start" in the three fundamental relationships. If you're beginning to love God, neighbor, or self in the midst of the struggle, you're winning.

One time Jesus' disciples were grumbling because they had forsaken all of their securities to follow Him and were afraid that others who had made lesser sacrifices would be rewarded more generously than they (Matthew 19:23-30).

Jesus responded by giving them His winning-is-beginning parable (Matthew 20:1-16). He said there was a man who went out early one morning to hire laborers to work in his vineyard. They agreed to work all day for one silver coin. At mid-morning, the boss went and hired some more. At noon he hired more. Then some more at mid-afternoon, and finally some at almost 5:00 P.M.

When it came time to pay all of the laborers, he paid each of them one silver coin, a full day's wages! Obviously the ones who worked the longest began to complain. "Listen," said the owner, "I haven't cheated you. I paid you the agreed wage. It's my vineyard and my money. Don't I have the right to spend my money as I please? Or are you jealous because I am generous?"

Jesus concluded, "So the last shall be first and the first shall be last in the kingdom." In other words, God doesn't separate the beginners from the finishers when he passes out the gold medals.

LOVING GOD

I long to love God the way some people tell of loving Him, but honestly, I seldom have those feelings.

I'm like the little boy who was afraid to sleep alone. When his mother assured him that God would be with him to protect and love him through the night, he said, "But I need somebody in here who has some skin on him!" It is hard to love someone who "has no skin on him" in the same way that you love people who do.

The good news is that you don't have to. Loving God with all your might has very little to do with *feeling* but has everything to do with *willing*. Be willing to trust Him, or rather, be willing *to start* to trust Him. Winning is beginning.

One of my favorite exchanges of Jesus with His disciples is the one He had with Simon Peter by the seashore after the Resurrection (John 21). Peter was the one who always ran his mouth before his head was in gear. (That's why I identify with him.) He promised to stand by Jesus no matter what. He even tried once to walk on water. But when Jesus was about to be executed, he denied Jesus three times.

After the Crucifixion, Simon leads the disciples back to a life of fishing. Then the Lord appears and feeds them breakfast by the sea at dawn. When they've finished eating, Jesus asks Peter, "Do you love me more than these other disciples do?" That had been Simon's boast for three years. Then Jesus asks a simple, "Do you love me?" two more times. Simon answers yes each time, but the last time, he breaks down. No doubt he remembers the three times he denied Jesus.

Every time Simon says, "Yes, I love you," Jesus simply replies, "Well, then, feed my sheep." Here's the point: *Simon doesn't have to love Jesus the "mostest" with the "bestest." All he has to do is love Jesus as much as he is able!*

Winning is beginning when it comes to loving God!

"Loving God with all your might has very little to do with feeling but has everything to do with willing."

LOVING OTHERS

I have as much difficulty *feeling* love toward strangers as I do feeling love toward a God "with no skin on him." How can you love a stranger as you love yourself?

There are only eight houses on the street where I live. The neighbors on my right and left are like my own family. They attend our church, and I couldn't have ordered better neighbors if I'd tried. Of the five remaining families on the block, I know the names of two.

Truthfully, I *feel* toward only two families as I *feel* toward my own. Am I a hypocrite? How can I call myself a Christian? Was Jesus simply trying to silence His critics with the neighbor-as-self bit? You will remember that when He said it, He was being taunted by the religious lawyers who wanted to make Him look bad. Perhaps He was simply trying to shut them up.

Well, I'm so glad that Luke adds an additional wrinkle to the story. In Matthew and Mark, the lawyers ask Jesus, "What is the greatest religious commandment of all?" When He answers, "Love God! And then love neighbor as self," that's the end of it. But in Luke one of the lawyers asks, "Who is my neighbor?"

Jesus answers with the famous parable of the Good Samaritan (Luke 10:25-37). There is no need to recount the parable, except to say that the only time "feeling" is mentioned is when the Samaritan sees the victim of the robbery lying in the ditch. It says, "his heart was filled with pity" (Luke 10:33). The word pity can also be translated "undeniable responsibility."

The Good Samaritan loved his neighbor as himself by simply deciding to be responsible for him in the hour of his need. He couldn't simply pass by.

POINT: *You don't have to be Mother Teresa to love your neighbor as yourself.* You don't have to renounce your fame and fortune and become an itinerant monk (unless, of course, God shows you that this is your way to live out His commandment to love).

To love your neighbor as yourself simply means to acknowledge your responsibility for the needs of others you encounter on the road of your life, and, of course, to render help according to your resources. If your resources are little, give a little. If a lot, give a lot. I fear that we ministers in our zeal for perfection sometimes lead people to believe that if they can't do everything for every problem in the entire world then they are less than neighborly in God's eyes. The result is the "I can't do everything, so I'll do nothing" syndrome.

The fiery prophet, John the Baptist, knew this. When it came to calling people to repentance, he was without peer. He thundered doom for the wicked. But when he "had them on the ropes," so to speak, he did not load them down with unreachable ideals.

When they asked what they could do in order to get right with God and avoid judgment, he gave them simple, concrete instructions (Luke 3). "Whoever has two shirts must give one to the man who has none and whoever has food must share it. [Tax collectors,] don't collect more than is legal. [Soldiers,] don't take money from anyone by force or accuse anyone falsely. Be content with your pay" (Luke 3:11-14).

When it comes to loving your neighbor as yourself, take small, practical baby-steps, and grow from there! Winning is beginning to do the little things for others that you would like them to do for you.

Kenneth Erickson's book, *The Power of Praise,* should be required reading for the human race. He says a creative mathematician figured out that if one person complimented two other persons each day and the recipients did likewise in geometrical progression, two million compliments could be passed around in twenty-one days![3] He also says that a female dog gives her pups nine gentlings for each nip or growl. With humans, it's almost the opposite.

Gert Behenna spoke to three thousand Baptist preachers at a

convention. She was in her seventies by then. First, she told the wonderful story of her conversion in a flophouse while she was alone and dying from alcohol poisoning. "Amens!" could be heard all across the large meeting hall.

"If you can't do everything, do one thing."

Then she lit a cigarette, took a deep drag, and exhaled the smoke toward the audience. Gasps replaced the amens. "I've been wanting to do that to Baptist preachers for years," she said. "And I'm glad I did it. Boy, it's worth the look on your faces!"

She paused and took another drag. Then she said, "You are now more offended by my smoking at a religious meeting than you are *thrilled* with my salvation!"

I had to meet this lady. She came to my church and spoke. By the end of the week, the place was filled with all kinds of "sinners." Some of the regulars were offended, but they still came.

We had one lady who had been campaigning for the "Mrs. Southern Baptist Convention" title for years. There was no such title, but she was in training just in case there ever was. She was disturbed by Gert, to say the least.

On the last day Gert was with us, we had a women's luncheon. During the question and answer session, Mrs. Southern Baptist Convention saw her opening. She asked, "How do you think a truly Christian woman can best glorify the Lord Jesus in this lost world of ours?"

Without the slightest pause, Gert answered, "Well, I don't know about a *truly* Christian woman, but I clean public toilets myself."

Everyone looked confused. "Whenever I'm at a public event where there's a large crowd using the rest rooms, I take paper towels and wipe off the lavatories and the floors. I pick up all of the paper. Then I polish the mirrors and wipe the toilet bowls. First thing you know, someone will ask me why I'm doing it. I tell 'em, 'In the name of Jesus.' That really does the trick. They want to know what Jesus has to do with cleaning toilets. I tell 'em He said, 'Love your neighbor as yourself.' Then I tell 'em how much I enjoy using a clean toilet and how I figured they would, too."

If you can't do everything, do one thing. I heard about a wife whose husband had a stressful job. She was adding to his stress by greeting him with problems the moment he came home every day—the kids' behavior or the bills or something that had broken.

One day she decided that she would start greeting him with nothing but good news. To her surprise she didn't have to fake any good news. Every day there was something positive to tell him. Their marriage was reborn.

But after a while she had to get creative. One day he walked in and she said, "Two of our three kids did not break their arms today and the IRS is auditing us for only three out of the last four years!"

In this world, winning means finishing the race first. In God's world, winning is beginning. Begin looking only for good news, and share it.

LOVING SELF

I am reluctant to mention self-love for a couple of reasons. First, we've already talked about self-esteem. Secondly, we've had more than enough books on the subject, some of which are designed to reinforce the spirit of self-indulgence which flourished in the 1960s through the 1980s.

So let me get directly to the point. To love yourself, as Jesus used the expression, means to see yourself as God sees you, to define yourself as God would define you.

And winning is beginning when it comes to seeing ourselves as God sees us! We shall never be able to shake off all of the low self-images with which we were branded as children. We shall never completely stop listening to the "liars" and to the little "child within" which I discussed in Chapter 6. The good news is that we do not have to. All it takes is a glimpse of who we are in God's eyes, and we begin to be winners in the struggle for self-esteem.

There's a fable about a boy who found an egg in the forest and brought it home to the barnyard. He placed it in the nest of a goose who was sitting on her own eggs. When the hatchlings emerged from their shells, the goslings were uniformly yellow and pretty. Out of the "foreign egg" came a dark brown, ugly creature with greasy feathers and twisted feet.

As the months passed and the hatchlings grew, the brown, gangly creature learned to walk and swim like the others. But his gait was awkward. He would almost drown in the pond. His honk was only a shriek.

Then one day as all of the fowl in the barnyard were enjoying themselves, a shadow passed over them. Chickens, geese, ducks, and guineas scurried for cover. But the creature wasn't afraid. He looked up and saw the bird of prey circling ominously. He began to run and flap his gangly wings.

Suddenly he left the ground. The wind began to lift him higher and higher toward the fearsome bird of prey. The fowl in the barnyard were weeping; they knew he would soon be dead.

But as he drew near the monstrous bird and could see his eyes, he found welcome and warmth in them. In a flash he knew. The great bird was a finished model of what he, the gangly creature, was meant to be.

You see, the creature was born an eagle, but he had been trying to live like a goose!

I'm saying that once you receive a glimpse of the way God intended you, you're a winner. But how do we receive that glimpse? One of my teammates in the ministry of our church helped me with this a few years ago, in a way I never expected.

"Big Charlie," we call him. He's about six feet five. Charlie came to our church as a successful business and family man who hadn't been to church since he was a child. Through an astonishing series of events, he has ended up as our executive pastor, which means he does everything I can't or don't want to do.

When Charlie was fifteen, his father was killed. Over the years, Charlie internalized the tragedy. (Remember, the child within thinks everything bad is his fault.) Somehow, he "had killed his father."

Al-Anon was Charlie's salvation for a long period of time. He went to meetings regularly, practiced the Twelve Steps of A.A., and found the community of help and healing which he desperately needed, even though there were no alcoholics in his immediate family.

One day I was telling Charlie about my continuing struggle to see myself as God sees me. I poured out the whole dirty business of not feeling I had received my father's blessing, of never feeling I had measured up, and of my infantile need for applause and the spotlight.

"I know that all of this stuff comes from not accepting God's acceptance of me," I said, "but I keep falling into the trap of letting the child within tell me who I am!" Then I blurted out, "I detest the little monster."

Charlie said, "I know how you feel. For years I have replayed in my mind the scene where my dad drove away for the last time. I watched him go and never saw him again. Before he left, I didn't tell him I loved him. For years I felt that if I had told him, he would have been more careful and not crashed his plane."

Then he said, "Let me tell you something I've been doing as a result of attending my Al-Anon group. I've been remembering the times in my childhood like the one I've just described—the times when I felt really rotten about myself. I go back and pick up little Charlie, and I love him. I caress him and hold him and forgive him.

"And you know what?" he continued. "The more I do this, the more little rotten Charlies I find—Charlies I have forgotten in my conscious mind. They are hidden away in cold dark corners everywhere. There are hundreds of the little beggars! One by one I seek them out and love them."

I started looking back in the dark corners of my past for the "little rotten Gerries." And there were many. I remembered when I was six and my dad put me on a deer stand in the woods before daylight on a cold morning and told me not to return to camp. "If I wanted to be a man," I would tough it out.

An armadillo came close to me. I panicked and ran back to camp. I was scolded for my cowardice. I was told that I was not a man.

I remembered refusing to fight the school bully because I was afraid. I was not a man.

I remembered the night I rushed for two hundred fifty yards and scored five touchdowns. On the last play of the game, I broke into the secondary and had the choice of cutting left or right. I chose the right and the defensive back made a touchdown-saving tackle. When I walked into the house, I was told, "Why didn't you turn left on the last play? You would have made six touchdowns and broken the state's single game rushing record!"

"You coulda done better, Gerry," is the credo which has dominated so much of my life.

Big Charlie's method has been a great gift to me, and I give it to you. Do you want to see yourself as God sees you? Travel backward into all of those cold, dark, rotten places in your past and find all of those little beggars. Pick them up. Caress and hug them one by one.

You're loving yourself when you do that. And you're loving God and your neighbor. I agree with those who say, "Thou shalt love thy neighbor as thyself" was not a commandment but a stated fact. You *will* love your neighbor just as you love yourself.

My purpose in all of this is to express my conviction that we cannot make the bad times over for good without loving God, neighbor, and self. And the good news is that we don't have to be perfect lovers. All we need is the heart to start. Winning is beginning.

And for those who have begun and failed, I need to add that winning is beginning, *again*.

YOU CAN BEGIN AGAIN!

On the first Sunday of every New Year I have given the same sermon for ten straight years. The people know it's coming, and they fill the place anyway.

"Intimacy means being fully known and fully accepted by another and fully safe all the time."

I begin with the old saw which says, "You can't change human nature." I say, "Oh, but you can!" Of all the things in nature, the human part is the most unpredictable and change-able. The rotation of planets and atoms doesn't change. Gravity is boringly redundant. But people change all the time.

After Broken Relationships

The thread which holds the sixty-six books of the Bible together is the possibility of new beginnings. The best news of all the good news is, "You can begin again!" There's as much a victory in beginning again as there is in beginning the first time.

You can begin again after broken relationships. Nothing hurts worse than the loss of that magic thing we call intimacy. Intimacy means being fully known and fully accepted by another and fully safe all the time.

To be able to show myself and give myself to another, and for that gift not to be used to hurt me or manipulate me, is what I crave in my deepest heart. And so do you.

When intimacy is shattered, part of us dies. Innocence is gone. The world will never be the same again. We're told we cannot go back to Eden. But the Bible says, "Oh, yes, we can!" Read the twenty-eighth book of the Old Testament, the book of an ancient struggler named Hosea. His wife left him and the kids to become a prostitute in a pagan temple.

As Hosea fumbled amid the wreckage of his hurt, God told him something like this: "Now you know how I feel. The people I love keep acting like whores, too. They sell themselves to other gods. But I keep buying them back."

Hosea takes everything he has and pays it to redeem his wife Gomer. He feels the same way about her as God feels about Israel: "How can I give you up, Israel? How can I abandon you?...My heart will not let me do it! My love for you is too strong" (Hosea 11:8).

Hosea and Gomer rebuild their relationship. Adultery is not the end. I have seen several instances over the years where sexual infidelity actually triggered a process which created a relationship that was stronger than before.

Please don't misunderstand. I'm not recommending adultery as a cure for a bad marriage any more than I'm recommending a bullet as a cure for a headache. I'm just saying that if relationships can be wrecked, they can also be rebuilt.

After Moral Failure

You can also begin again after moral failure—after you've done the very thing you said you'd never do, after you've compromised the last shred of your integrity.

Who hasn't heard of the great moral collapse of King David? It had all of the scandal and juice of a supermarket tabloid—hanky-panky, adultery, out-of-wedlock pregnancy, murder, intrigue in the royal court.

The postman rang twice, and his name was Nathan the prophet. David was caught red-handed. He had been trained by Samuel. He had refused to assassinate King Saul. He had unified the empire. He had written the Psalms. Yet in one moral lapse, he had compromised a wondrous life.

But speaking of the Psalms, have you ever read the fifty-first? It stands as a monument to David's moral recovery. David began again. He didn't try to cover up. He didn't pass the guilt to his underlings. Nor did he issue a public statement admitting to "poor judgment."

He started with God, with a power capable of creating within him a new heart (Psalm 51:10). He needed more than confession; he needed a moral transplant.

As you know, Bathsheba's baby was stillborn. But that wasn't the end of the story.

I am amused at how often one of the key lessons about David is forgotten. For instance, a couple of years ago I read the transcript of a forum held by some of America's leading radio and TV preachers. They were addressing the subject of whether a minister who has committed adultery should ever be restored to his former professional status.

One popular evangelical radio preacher and biblical scholar said that fallen ministers should be forgiven but not restored to pastoral responsibilities. And he used David as his biblical proof! David, according to Mr. Radio, was never as spiritually effective after his sin with Bathsheba.

Hasn't he heard of Solomon? Well, his mother was Bathsheba and his father was David. Where did Solomon's wisdom come from? And his fierce integrity? And his appreciation for the beauty of a love between man and woman which fuses the physical with the spiritual? (The Song of Solomon).

In his old age, David had to pay the price of neglecting personal relationships with several of his family and associates. But he raised a great son out of the ashes of moral failure.

You can begin again after moral failures. I keep one of Pascal's sayings near me at all times:

> In all the world there are only two kinds of people. The vast majority, sinners, who believe themselves saints, and the rest, saints, who believe themselves sinners.[4]

After Broken Dreams

You can begin again after great disappointments as well. Remember Elijah? His lifelong dream was to see his countrymen shed their false gods and follow only Yahweh.

Jezebel, the queen, had different ideas. She had the priests of Baal set up shop in the royal court and build altars on holy Mount Carmel.

Elijah goaded her and the priests into a duel and won. The entire country rallied to God, overturned the icons of Baal, and slew his priests. But the revival lasted only a few hours. The crowd turned into a lynch mob. Jezebel's forces were scouring the countryside for Elijah.

He hid in a cave and asked to die. His life's dream was shattered. He fell into a full-fledged clinical depression—wouldn't eat, wouldn't talk, withdrew into himself, "heard voices" in the wind, the lightning, and the earthquake. But the voices weren't God's. God's voice was in "the silence." I know, the verse has been translated to read that God spoke to him in a "still small voice" (1 Kings 19:12, NKJV). It can also be translated "in the silence."

After the silence, Elijah "stood at the entrance of the cave" (1 Kings 19:13). *He came out of his cave! Then he heard God's voice!*

And what did he hear from God? "Get yourself up, Elijah! Return to your dream! Anoint. Speak! You are not the last faithful person left on this earth! You can begin again after broken dreams!"

Every New Year's Day I read a condensed chronology of Abraham Lincoln's life.[5]

- 1832 Lost job and defeated for legislature
- 1833 Failed in business
- 1834 Elected to legislature
- 1835 Sweetheart died
- 1836 Had a nervous breakdown
- 1838 Defeated for speaker
- 1843 Defeated for nomination to Congress
- 1846 Elected to Congress
- 1848 Lost renomination
- 1849 Rejected for land officer
- 1854 Defeated for Senate
- 1856 Defeated for nomination to vice president
- 1858 Again, defeated for Senate
- 1860 Elected president of the United States

You get the idea that God wanted Lincoln to be president. I'm glad Lincoln wasn't like Isadore McIngle. Never heard of him? I hadn't either until I heard Robert Schuller talk about him. According to Schuller, a father was quizzing his son on his history lessons.

"The world loves a winner.
God loves a beginner."

"Son," he said, "have you ever heard of Thomas Jefferson, Andrew Jackson, and George Washington?"

"Sure," said the boy. "They were all presidents."

"Do you know another reason why you've heard of 'em?" asked the dad. "They never quit! Now, let me ask if you've heard of Isadore McIngle."

"No," said the lad.

"See! He quit!"

The world loves a winner. God loves a beginner. "Except ye return and become as children," said Jesus. God loves people who make little baby steps in loving Him and their neighbors and themselves. And God loves "begin againers."

Where to Begin Again

Are you asking, "Where do I begin to begin?" "Where do I get the heart to start?" "How do I begin again?" I can tell you what works for me. I do three things. First, I identify my "If onlies," and add "next times" to them. I go back and dredge up all of the things I wish I had done differently and all of the things I wish I hadn't done at all.

When I've written down all of the regrets of my past, I take a big red marker and write in big letters across the page, *next time!*

You see, the good news of Jesus Christ is that you can turn all of your "if onlies" into "next times." Even the terminally ill can write *next time* after, "if only I didn't have cancer."

Bereaved parents who've lost their children can write *next time* after their "if onlies." There is another life beyond this one. Death is an exit and an entrance. We *shall* meet again. There is no "if only" without a "next time."

The second thing I do is identify all of my "what if's" and add "so what's" to them. "If onlies" have to do with the past; "what if's" have to do with the future.

The gospel's answer to "what if" is "so what!" So I write down all of my fears regularly. And after I've read over them several times, I get the green marker. Green stands for go; red stands for stop. I write "So What!" across all of my "what-if's."

The third thing I do is "knock the T out of my can'ts." I had a junior high coach who was a master motivator. Before every game, he would write "can't" in big letters across the chalk board. He'd say, "Men, this is what the odds and the other team and the newspapers are saying about us today. Now, what are we gonna go out there and do?"

We'd shout in unison, "Knock the T out of can't!"

These little games I play are more than games. They are rituals for reminding me of the life-giving grace of God that is available to me every day. To trade my "if onlies" for "next times" is to let go of my past and leave it to God. To trade my "what-if's" for "so what's" is to give my future to God. To knock the T out of my "can'ts" is to give today to God.

Jesus said, "If anyone desires to come after Me, let him deny himself, take up his cross, and follow Me" (Matthew 16:24, NKJV). For a long time, this saying seemed too harsh to me. It seemed to say that following Christ was an austere, self-hating, painful exercise. Here's an other version: "If anyone wants to come and experience the joy of life that I experience, let him deny all of those guilt-ridden false images of his past which torture him; and let him daily nail these lies to the Cross; and let him follow Me into the future without fear." Jesus' invitation is not to a life of self-mutilation but an invitation to joy.

I once heard a story about G. K. Chesterton who was on a picnic with his granddaughter in the springtime. He was bouncing the little girl on his knee, and every time he bounced her, she would giggle and say the three words kids say: "Do it again!" First a bounce, then a "Do it again!" This went on until they were both exhausted, and the little girl went off to play.

Chesterton began to study in detail the scene before him and to smile to himself as he thought of his granddaughter. Then the thought struck him that God had not made children or the field of daisies in front of him all at once. He had created them one at a time. And each time He created one, He had giggled with delight and said to Himself, "Do it again!"

When He finished with daisies, God went to daffodils, thought Chesterton. *And then roses, and then every flower on earth one at a time! And then animals.*

Then Chesterton imagined God creating people. One by one God had created every single human who ever lived. And each and every time He giggled with delight and said, "Do it again! Do it again!"

Of course, Chesterton eventually got around to the most stupendous thought: God had gotten around to him. He was a product of God's delightful "Do it again!"

When God made you and me, He giggled and said "Do it again!" He didn't have "humankind" in mind when He made you. He had *you* in mind! If only we could begin to get in touch with that stupendous fact. Winning is beginning.

9

The Little Path Is the Middle Path

Ever since Jesus said the way that leads to life is the "narrow way" (Matthew 7:13), many of us have tended to interpret the Christian life in negative terms. *Narrow* has come to mean narrow-minded and narrow-visioned. The "way to life" has been interpreted primarily as an exercise in subtraction—the more enjoyment you can subtract from your life, the closer you come to God.

I fell into this mentality soon after hooking up with the Baptists. Although I didn't realize it at the time, I received considerable pride and applause for ridding my life of "unchristian behavior"—which included everything from smoking to laughing at jokes.

I was sorting through old sermon notes not long ago and happened upon one from 1960, when I was twenty-two. The title was, "How to Stay the Narrow Way." (All good sermon titles must rhyme, you know.) Here's an excerpt:

> Read your Bible instead of watching TV. Cut your
> sleep thirty minutes a day and pray instead. Don't

speak to strangers unless you plan to ask them if they're saved. Don't buy food where liquor is sold. Boycott all school activities until the school board stops meeting during Wednesday night prayer meeting.

I won't bore you further except to say, one day it occurred to me that if the "narrow way" were the way of subtraction, then the most dedicated Christian would be the person who achieved a state of suspended animation. In fact, I knew a Tibetan monk who claimed to have accomplished precisely that.

Some years later I wrote a book on Jesus' Sermon on the Mount (Matthew 5-7).[1] When I worked through the part which we now call Matthew 7, I discovered something that would forever change my life: *The narrow way that leads to life is not the way of the extreme "right" or of the extreme "left." It is the way of the middle.*

Throughout Jesus' life extremists were trying to enlist Him. The old-line conservative establishment, represented by the Pharisees, sent Nicodemus to recruit Him. The liberal establishment, represented by the Sadducees, were constantly baiting Him. The radical socio-political Zealots wanted Him to take up the sword. Cults on the emotional fringe, like the Essenes, who probably championed John the Baptist, asked if Jesus would be their Messiah or if they should look for another.

Jesus allowed Himself to be taught by all of these traditions, but to be "bought" by none of them. I am amazed at how seldom we are reminded of the political and social motives behind Jesus' death. He tried to universalize the faith of Israel, to take it to all people. The God of Abraham was not just for Jews or for one religious party of Jews or for one economic or moral or political stratum of Jewish society. God intended to love the entire world into a relationship with Himself.

When I say the narrow way is the way of the middle, I don't mean watered-down, mediocre religion that believes nothing

and therefore falls for everything. In Texas, we have a saying, "The middle of the road is for yellow stripes and dead armadillos"—cowards and confused varmints. That's mostly true.

But there's another way to look at the middle of the road. The yellow stripe stands for risk and danger. The reason there are dead critters there is because they are getting hit from both sides, from folks on the left and on the right. On any given issue—especially religious issues— you can always find plenty of company on the right and the left. But the way of the middle is a dangerous place to take your stand.

I think of the middle as the tightrope—that thin, shaky margin which hangs above made-up minds. Jesus did life from the tightrope.

In 1859, Charles Blondin, a French aerialist, strung a high wire 1300 feet across Niagara Falls. He drew a huge crowd and then proceeded to make his way across the chasm.

When he reached the halfway point, he stopped and sat. Then he lowered a rope to a boat waiting 190 feet below, hauled up a bottle of water, drank it, and resumed his stroll, reaching the other side without mishap.[2]

Jesus did life this way. He used skill, clear thinking, and derring-do. He lived on the tightrope. Like Blondin, He wasn't some "crazy fool." He knew what He was doing; He was in total control. He never exceeded His limits, but He pushed Himself to the edge of them.

The little path, the narrow way to life, is the middle path between absolutes. I know of no other principle more crucial than this when it comes to transforming trouble into triumph. First, I'll relate it to three areas of active religious life. Then I want us to see how Jesus used it to face His own suffering.

THE LITTLE PATH OF WORSHIP

Religious activity has no value if it does not empower us to metabolize both the little and the large pains of life. Worship,

for example, should be an experience which builds backbone. When God's people gather, one result should be the nerve to lift up our heads and go forward into the week. Sunday is not the end of the week; it's the launching pad. So whatever else worship should do for us, it should light the fire to reach higher.

The problem with most planners of worship is they forget that the little path is the middle path. We seem to be pulled in opposite directions when it comes to worship. Some of us want to reduce it to a "head trip." Everything must be proper and rational. The worship leaders are garbed in the vestments of long-gone centuries. Their language reverts to ancient incantational tones. They stand sideways in the pulpit and look bilious. Their sermons sound like something right out of a "reasoning with the child" seminar. Much time is spent re-explaining all of the symbols which are hanging around the sanctuary.

Someone needs to remind us that head-to-head worship doesn't help hurting people make it through the night. Hurters need heart-to-heart worship experiences. They want to *feel*. Reciting the Apostles' Creed and reading the lesson of the day is good indoctrination, but it's short on vitalization.

Then there are the groups who reduce worship exclusively to a "heart trip." The "hoop 'n' holler" groups are the fastest growing Christian churches in the world today. From South America to Korea to Africa to blue-collar U.S.A., people are "feeling" their worship experiences again. If they have to choose between worship as reasoning and worship as ecstasy, "hoop 'n' holler" will win every time.

I am not poking fun here. I'd take religion with feeling over the purely rational stuff any day. I'd rather have cotton candy and a carnival than prunes and a nap!

But these aren't the only two choices! The little path is the middle path in worship. There's no worship if people can't laugh and cry, and there's no worship if people must check

their brains at the door.

At our church, we try to give people two things at every worship service. They are represented by the acronyms G.O.D. and D.O.G.

G.O.D. is "gift of delight." Everyone who comes to Riverbend is given delight. We don't "mark" our visitors. That's because many people come to worship wounded. They want to be in a safe, non-threatening environment, but they don't want to be singled out. So we simply stop the service at different times and have everyone turn around and greet the person behind them. A smile and a handshake—that's what everyone is guaranteed at Riverbend.

In our children's ministry, smiles and hugs are a priority. The kids get those before they get anything else. The best way to give a person God is to give them G.O.D.—the gift of delight. It means, "We're glad you're you and nobody else, and you are welcome here whether you're like us or not!"

We give the gift of delight in other ways. I don't use a pulpit; I stand on a six-foot square box in the middle of my people. I don't use notes; I sit on a stool. I want nothing *between* me and the people. The threatening symbols of my being a "parent figure" are removed. One entire side of the room is clear glass through which the people can see the hill country and Lake Austin.

We also sing music which the people know and like. The instruments are piano, brass, and a guitar. People will always sing if they know and like the tune and if no one else can hear them. I don't know anyone who doesn't sing or at least hum in the shower. Why? Because the shower invites you to sing! The acoustics are great. The running water is your accompaniment.

> **"The best way to give a person God is to give them G.O.D.—the gift of delight."**

In many churches, the instrument used is the same one they use at funerals. The acoustics are dead. The tunes were made to listen to, not sing.

G.O.D. is our "heart" gift. People don't need sermons; they need handles of hope, help, and home. We often say, "If our worship service doesn't light your fire, your wood's wet." Sometimes it's an idle boast, but we work at it.

D.O.G. stands for "discovery of gifts." If religious activity is just a weekly dose of "feel-good" at worship on Sunday, it's of little value in making the world a better place. Each person has unique gifts. We've heard enough about that. But we haven't heard enough about helping people discover their gifts so that they can put them to use outside the church, where it counts.

This is where the rational side of religion is important. You have to think to find your gifts and use them. Religion needs to make sense where people live and work six days a week. How do you explain the death of a child to a mother without using your head? How do you explain to a teenager that the world is much bigger than her desire to be elected cheerleader without a rational world view? How do you explain the Christian world view to people who are being bombarded by other world views daily?

A faith that cannot harmonize the enormous influx of new information that hits us every day is useless.

Twenty-five years ago I heard Paul Tillich was coming to town. Tillich was one of the premier religious thinkers in the world. He had found ways to explain a rational faith to the worst of the skeptics. Most of my colleagues thought he was a rank heretic; I did, too, until I actually read his books.

I went early and got a front row seat. A disheveled, bookish sort of man came in and sat beside me. He greeted me and began to shuffle through some papers. After a moment, he turned to shake my hand. It was Paul Tillich!

Later, after the hall had filled, we all stood to sing a hymn before Tillich spoke. We sang "It Is Well with My Soul." We got to the verse which says, "Oh, Lord, haste the day when faith shall be sight . . . The clouds be rolled back like a scroll. The trump shall resound and the Lord shall descend..."

When we hit the high note on "descend," I felt my hand being squeezed. I looked over and Tillich was singing with all his might. Tears were on his cheeks.

Here was a man who had brought his heart *and* his head to worship. The little path that leads to life in worship is the middle path between religion which would reduce itself to feeling on the one hand or reason on the other.

THE LITTLE PATH OF WITNESSING

How do you tell others about your faith? Your religious values will come out in some way. How do you show yours?

Again there are two extremes. One is to conform to culture. That's where you change God to fit the current popular cause. Or more often it's where you figure a way to get God to endorse your life-style.

The other extreme is to curse culture. That's where you pronounce the world evil and unsalvageable and withdraw from it. "Come out from among them and be separate" (2 Corinthians 6:17, NKJV) is a favorite verse among culture-cursers. Now and then they dash out into the world to gather scalps for Jesus, but most faithing gets done inside the walls of the "holy community."

Jesus came in between these extremes. He immersed Himself in "the world." He could be found among the thieves and prostitutes and tax collectors. But He could also be found among the "up and ins." To portray Jesus as the champion of *only* one class or social stratum is a distortion. His relationships ranged from priests to paupers, from lepers to luxuriating snobs, from soldiers to shepherds, from princes to prostitutes.

He was truly cosmopolitan.

In fact, the record is clear that He got into trouble with the religious establishment for hanging out with a bad crowd. We all know the three lovely stories He told in Luke 15 about the lost sheep, the lost coin, and the lost son. Don't forget what prompted them. "The Pharisees . . . started grumbling, 'This man welcomes outcasts and even eats with them!' So Jesus told them this parable" (Luke 15:2-3).

Jesus went to the hurting people. He didn't withdraw and call them to come to Him. Then what?

First, He loved. That means He came to people unarmed. There was no judgment in Him. People were comfortable around Him.

Look how He treated the "sinners." He took away their defenses. "Zacchaeus [the tax collector and traitor], let's have lunch!" He said. To the prostitute He saved from stoning, "I don't condemn you either," He said. To love meant to establish an atmosphere of nonjudgmental acceptance. Jesus came unarmed.

Then He "let be," He *released* them to be what they didn't know they could be. To let be is to free people to become the selves they have lost sight of.

My grandmother was the most influential person in my spiritual formation as a child. She gave me both G.O.D. and D.O.G. She took great delight in me.

"Now, let's have a look at ya," was the way she greeted me. She would take my face between her hands and look into my eyes while her eyes danced with delight. She read Aesop to me, and Homer and Churchill and Dickens.

When I was sixteen, my parents went on a month-long trip. "Big Mama," as we called her, came to keep me. (She was all of four feet eleven inches tall.) Big Mama set her clock by the chickens. By 7:00 P.M., she was in bed.

On the first Saturday night of her stay, a pal and I got dates with the girls most often mentioned in the locker room. An older friend bought us a bottle which we stashed in a safe place. We were ready for our first foray into "sin."

As I was dressing, Big Mama came into the room, sat down on the bed, and watched me. I could see her in the mirror. She just sat there with this peculiar smile on her face. *Was it a knowing smile?* I wondered.

After a while, I grew nervous. "What are you grinning at?" I asked. "Oh, nothing," she said. "I'm sorry. I didn't mean to stare. I was just sitting here, thinking an old woman's thoughts."

"What thoughts?" I said, trying to sound casual.

"Oh, you wouldn't understand," she said. "Forget it."

"No, I wanta know," I persisted.

"Okay," she said. "I was just sitting here praising God under my breath. I was thanking Him for allowing me to live long enough to see you grow into such a fine young man. I have friends, you know, who couldn't be left alone for a month with their grandchildren. But your folks can go away and leave you with me without one fear. I was just praising God for the joy of watching you get ready. I'm going off to bed now, son. You have a wonderful time."

She ruined my night! I was home by 11:00, sober as a judge. The girls who would, didn't!

Big Mama was practicing the art of "letting be." She released me to be loyal to the royal in myself. She called me to reach to the higher part of me that was there all along. We hear a lot about saying no to the "beasts in our basement." I think we need to hear more about saying yes to the "angel in our attic."

A woman in our church came to see me. She was one of the most beloved and admired in our church family. "Twenty years ago, I committed adultery," she blurted out. I was stunned.

"I know you don't believe it, but it's true. It was a one-time thing. We both regretted it. I've been living with it for all of these years. It's eating me up. Should I tell my husband?"

I was younger then; I had such little experience. I told her to pray about it, and if she felt like it, to tell all to her husband.

In a couple of days she called. "I'm going to tell Bob (not his name) when he comes home tonight," she said. "If everything blows up, I'll know you gave me bad advice." Before I could get my breath, she rang off.

The next day she called. "You're wonderful!" she exclaimed. "I told Bob everything. He just smiled and said he'd known about it all along. He's just been waiting for me to tell him."

The little path is the middle when it comes to sharing our faith with others. We don't have to conform to culture or to curse it. Just love and let be.

At our church we believe that our task is to create an atmosphere of safety. We come to people unarmed. Once they feel safe and accepted, they let down their defenses. Hundreds *ask us* to baptize them every year. You see, people want to be made whole, but they don't want to be made over according to somebody else's prescription for wholeness.

"We don't have to conform to culture or to curse it. Just love and let be."

THE LITTLE PATH OF GOD'S WILL

"How can I know God's will for my life?" Who hasn't asked that question? It is frequently asked by people whose lives have been struck by suffering. When it comes to knowing God's will for our lives, there are two extremes as well. On the one hand, some people simply do what they're told by the preacher and the Bible according to the preacher— blind obedience without question. On the other extreme, some people walk only by sight. Unless they hear voices or "see handwriting," they do as they please. Of course, they don't do much as a result.

The little path that leads to life is the tightrope between walking by faith and walking by sight. Most of my Christian pilgrimage has been by faith. I have rarely known God's will beyond the shadow of a doubt. I have had to get by on glimpses and tugs and nudges. But without them I could not make it.

Here's an example of one of those glimpses. In the summer of 1961, I had finished my first year of seminary and knew that Cindy had to start to speech and hearing school in Houston by September. The choice appeared to be between continuing my schooling or continuing hers. Obviously, she came first. Yet I knew God had called me to the ministry, and I was convinced that I should continue my education.

The last week of August we packed up and headed for Houston. We moved in with my parents until I could find work and a place to live. My seminary days were over, so it seemed.

My mother, who attended Sunday school at a nearby church about three times a year, had been in class the day before we arrived. When we pulled up to her house, she came out to meet us. "I got you a place to preach this Sunday!" She went on to explain that her Sunday school teacher's brother was the chairman of a pulpit search committee at a small church outside of Houston. They needed a preacher the following Sunday, so Mom volunteered my services. She also told them I was great and unemployed.

I preached that Sunday. I was never worse, but I did manage to inform them that I needed a church.

The week passed and I waited. On Friday I shut myself

inside Mom's sewing closet with a little lamp and my Bible. I played the "jab and hope" game. That's where you jab your finger into the closed Bible, open it, and hope to find God's personal miraculous word for your problem.

I jabbed Leviticus 13:3. It consists of God's instructions to Moses on how to treat people with boils! "If the hairs in the boil are white, it's a dreaded disease," says verse 3. "If they are not white, it's not dreaded."

So much for jab and hope. I decided to pray, but I couldn't. So I decided to listen. A Scripture verse burned itself into my mind: "For your heavenly Father knows that you need all these things" (Matthew 5:32, NKJV). I came out of the closet.

The church asked me back to preach. Then they asked me to be their pastor. I accepted on the condition that they allow me to continue my schooling, three hundred miles away. They agreed, provided that I could be there for midweek services.

I agreed without the foggiest idea of how I could do it. Seminary classes are held Tuesday through Friday. I could travel by car on Mondays, but to go round trip for Wednesday seemed impossible. "Your Father knows what you need." Those words kept rolling over in my mind.

There were two airlines that made the Houston-Dallas route in those days. One was big; the other was Trans Texas Airways. They had a couple of turbo props and several military surplus DC-3 tail-draggers.

I parked outside the office of TTA president R. E. McConn. The receptionist and I went through the usual routine. Did I have an appointment? No. What was the nature of my business? Personal. Could I give her a clue? No. Mr. McConn was a busy man. I'd wait. I probably couldn't see him today. I'd come back every day until I did. I was not crazy, by the way. My uncle Frank was the long-time city councilman in Houston and would vouch for me.

That got me into McConn's office. He got straight to it—

what did I want? "A free pass on your airline to travel back and forth from Houston to Dallas so that I can complete my education for the ministry and my deaf daughter can learn to talk." I said it all in one breath.

"You must be crazy!" he said. "No, sir. I'm desperate. I came to you because you know what it's like to be desperate. No one could start an airline with surplus DC-3's and not know what it's like to be desperate."

"I cannot give free passes on the airline," he said. "It's against the law. No one except employees can fly non-revenue."

"Well, give me a job," I said.

"What can you do?" he said.

"Whatever needs doing from Houston to Dallas and back on Tuesdays, Wednesdays, and Fridays while I'm in the air," I replied. "I have no time otherwise."

I walked out of his office with a sixty-dollar-a-month job and a free pass on his airline. My job? I was a "sky spy." I flew incognito and checked things out. I filled out a form of twelve questions each of which could be checked in a yes and no box. "Did the plane leave on time?" Yes or no. "Was the stewardess friendly?" Yes or no.

Soon most of the employees knew who I was, and they hated me. I solved that by writing nothing but good reports on everyone!

One morning I was the only passenger. The copilot and the stewardess smooched all the way to Dallas. Maybe they did more; my view was partially obstructed.

In my report when I came to the part entitled, "Evaluation of Stewardess," I wrote, "This girl is very good at what she does."

The employees came to love me. I flew to and from school for the next seven years. On the very same day that I returned from submitting my doctoral dissertation, there was a letter in the mail from R. E. McConn, Jr., who had succeeded his father as CEO. Trans Texas Airways had sold out, and he regretted to inform me that our arrangement would have to be terminated.

Most of the time I have to walk by faith instead of sight, but there have been those unmistakable glimpses. They are enough. "Your Father knows what you need before you ask Him."

The little path is the middle path when it comes to worship, witnessing, and discerning God's will. People who transform trouble into triumph are the ones who travel the tightrope between extremes. I want to turn now to an example of how Jesus Himself used the tightrope principle to face His most crucial night of suffering.

HOW JESUS MADE IT THROUGH THE NIGHT

Jesus responded to His impending death in much the same way as we ordinary mortals do. He knew it was the night before the Cross. Judas had gone to betray Him, and the clock was running out. What He had known was going to happen was now in fact unfolding.

He went to a garden outside of Jerusalem called Gethsemane. You can read about the sequence of events in Mark 14:32ff.

Between Panic and Perseverance

First, He tells His disciples to wait for Him while He goes into the garden to pray. Then He draws aside His three closest friends, Peter, James, and John.

The text says, "Distress and anguish came over him, and he said to them, 'The sorrow in my heart is so great that it almost crushes me'" (Mark 14:33-34).

Even though He had known what was coming, He still was not ready for it! His chest felt as if it would burst. He reached out to His friends in a desperate attempt for support against the inevitable. In a word, Jesus reacted to tragedy the same way we do.

But on the other hand, He knew He had to do His own grieving. His friends could support Him, but they couldn't do His dying for Him. So He told them, "Stay here and keep watch," and He went on to be alone (Mark 14:34).

Here's the tightrope, the narrow way, the little path of suffering—the little path between panic and perseverance. Jesus almost panicked, but He persevered.

> **POINT:** It's okay to fall apart and bleed on your friends. Jesus did! But in the end, you must do your own grieving.

Between Begging and Bending

So Jesus goes on alone to deal with *His* death *His* way. Then He does another thing which is altogether normal for any human. The text says, "[He] threw himself on the ground and prayed that, if possible, he might not have to go through that time of suffering" (Mark 14:35).

"'Father,' he prayed, 'my Father! All things are possible for you. Take this cup of suffering away from me'" (Mark 14:36).

> **POINT:** It's okay to bargain and beg when life tumbles in. Jesus did!

My dear friend Charlie Shedd and I talked almost every day while his beloved Martha was dying of cancer. We begged and bargained and screamed and cried together by long distance telephone. Every day we prayed for a miracle of healing.

On Ash Wednesday before Easter, Charlie said, "It appears

that Martha may not get her miracle of healing from cancer. So we are praying for her *ultimate healing* by Easter." The day before Easter, Martha went to heaven. She had the miracle of ultimate healing on Resurrection day.

Jesus walked between begging and bending, for in the next breath after pleading for relief, He said to God, "Yet, not what I want, but what You want" (Mark 14:36). He was willing to go through the veil of suffering to the "ultimate healing." He asked not to, but He didn't waver.

Between Activity and Acceptance

Jesus now comes out of the garden and finds His disciples asleep. He scolds them. Here He is in His worst moment, and they are sleeping!

The following verses picture Jesus as a frenetic figure, running back and forth between the garden and the disciples (Mark 14:37-41). He runs to pray, returns to And the disciples sleeping, scolds them, and runs back to pray.

Again, I'm glad this scene was not deleted from Scripture, because Jesus is doing all of the normal things we do in the face of suffering.

He quickens His activity to an almost feverish pace. He wants to *do something* to fix it!

> **POINT:** It s okay to become agitated and to rush after solutions when life tumbles in. Jesus did!

But in the end He walks the "little middle" between activity and acceptance. "Enough!" He says. "The hour has come.... Get up! Let us go" (Mark 14:41-42).

Jesus made it through the night of suffering by balancing on the tightrope between panic and perseverance, between begging and bending, and between activity and acceptance. He was indeed fully human, experiencing all of the temptations of allowing trouble to paralyze Him.

He resisted them by refusing to be sucked into extremes. He followed the little path that leads through the darkness to the day, to the "ultimate healing."

The little path is the middle path, and few there are who find it.

10

There's Clout in Doubt

There are some stories that make me laugh no matter how many times I think of them. To my dismay, others don't regard them the same way. You've probably heard this one, but I like to tell it anyway.

A televangelist went snow skiing. He was rather full of himself so he refused to take lessons. He simply strapped on the skis, mounted the ski lift, and headed for the top of the mountain.

He passed the green station marking the spot where less experienced skiers disembarked. Then he passed the blue and didn't get off until he reached the turnaround at the black station.

Off of the chair he came. Down the hill he flew, end over end to the first turn, which he didn't take. He sailed over a cliff into a yawning gorge. About ten feet down, he miraculously grabbed a tree branch. There he hung, suspended over certain death.

He yelled at the top of his lungs, "Is anybody up there?" It so happened that a renowned "liberal" minister, who caught constant flak from the televangelist for his "godless" beliefs, had witnessed the entire scene.

The liberal stayed out of the televangelist's view and called down to him. "Yes, there is someone up here," he said in a disguised voice. "It is I, the Lord your God. The time of your testing is at hand. If you truly believe as you so often proclaim, simply let go and I shall send my angels to catch thee."

There was a pregnant silence from below. Then came the haunting question, "Is anybody else up there?"

We would all like to really let go and trust God, wouldn't we? But we'd like something more substantial than a disembodied voice to go on.

Among the things I've been trying to say throughout this book is that we can trust God to support us in making the bad times over for the good, that we truly can let go of our fears of the past and the future.

But there is always doubt, isn't there? No matter how much we deny it, we are born skeptics. In the early years of my ministry, I felt threatened by anyone who expressed doubts about God's existence and goodness. I would go on the attack if someone asked a simple question about the trustworthiness of the biblical record.

There was one fellow at the little Baptist college where I enrolled following my conversion who prided himself in deflating the ardent claims of the preacher-boys at the school. He had read a little philosophy and some history of how the Bible was originally organized. He knew enough to give all of us beginners in the faith holy fits.

He would tie us in such intellectual knots that sometimes our only line of defense was to pronounce hellfire on him. "You're an infidel bound for hell" was said to him more than once. I am sorry to say that I went beyond that and punched the guy one day.

Spitting blood, he grinned, and said, "Doubt just scares the hell out of you, doesn't it?" He had kayoed me!

I believe that much of the bitter criticism that is aimed by religious figures at people who don't share their beliefs is the result of a masked fear over hidden doubt. We are mortified to admit to ourselves that we cannot shake those lurking doubts.

What if all of our claims are, in fact, convenient fictions? What if God is not? What if the miracles in the Bible are simply an accumulation of folk tales not unlike the myths which we so quickly identify in other major religions?

More pertinent to our purpose in this book, what if suffering is the final proof that life is a tale told by an idiot, and we are alone on this tiny speck of dust, hurtling through the dead void?

I can only say that one of the most liberating moments of my life was the moment when I was no longer afraid to ask those questions honestly. In a strange way, doubt has been my best companion throughout my search for the light in the darkness.

There's clout in doubt is how I put it. The Bible acknowledges this. Some of the biblical characters were plagued by doubt. Abraham made a covenant with God and immediately gave his wife to Pharaoh because he doubted that God would protect him in a foreign land.

> **"We are mortified to admit to ourselves that we cannot shake those lurking doubts.... What if all of our claims are, in fact, convenient fictions? What if God is not? What if the miracles in the Bible are simply an accumulation of folk tales?"**

Jacob had a vision where God promised to bless him. But he "hedged his bets" by stealing everything he could.

The book of Job is about a man who uses his doubt as a stepping-stone to a rock-solid faith. Ecclesiastes pulls no punches concerning doubt. The writer begins with the outright declaration that all of life is foolish and useless. "I've seen everything done in this world," he says, "and I tell you it is all useless" (Ecclesiastes 1:14). Later he says, "It is better to go to a home where there is mourning than to one where there is a party, because the living should always remind themselves that death is waiting for us all" (Ecclesiastes 7:2).

Yet at the end of his mournful trek through life's absurdities, the philosopher of Ecclesiastes concludes that we should work hard, honor God, and enjoy His gifts to the fullest for the brief time we have them. "Have reverence for God, and obey his commands, because this is all that man was created for" (Ecclesiastes 12:13). The philosopher did not have the hope of the afterlife as we do, yet even for him there was clout in doubt.

Which brings me to the man in the New Testament whose name has been most often associated with doubt: Thomas, one of Jesus' disciples. I think he's been given a bad rap because his doubting led him to the real thing.

You remember his story. He was always the realist and the questioner. When Jesus announces that He is going to Bethany to raise His friend Lazarus from the dead in order to prove to the disciples that He is the Messiah, the disciples are skeptical.

Thomas says sarcastically, "Let's all go along with the Teacher, so that we may die with him." He thinks the whole business is absurd, but he's willing to go check it out (John 11:16).

On the last night when Jesus tells the group that he is going to the Father and they know the way, Thomas says, "Lord, we do not know where you are going" (John 14:5).

When Jesus first appeared to His disciples after the Resurrection, Thomas wasn't there. When they told him, he replied, "Unless I see the scars of the nails in his hands and put my finger on these scars and my hand in his side, I will not believe" (John 20:24-25). Jesus appears to him and invites him to touch His wounds. Only then does Thomas reply, "My Lord and my God!" (John 20:28).

I have mentioned these encounters because they stand as vivid examples of the clout in doubt. Thomas's doubting led him to certainty and will lead us there as well.

COURAGEOUS DOUBT

There are two kinds of doubt. One kind doubts everything because it is convenient. He who is certain of nothing commits to nothing. The easy way to slide through life uncommitted is to be an intellectual dilettante who dabbles in every philosophy but believes in none.

But then there is Thomas's doubt, the courageous kind, the kind that separates what it wishes were true from what it actually sees as true. Thomas wished that Jesus could raise Lazarus from the dead, but he refused to settle for the wishful. He had to see it. He wished that the report of Jesus' resurrection were true, but he refused to allow his wish to blur the reality of fact. Unless he could bolster his desires with personal verification, he would not believe.

Never be afraid to demand firsthand verification. If Thomas hadn't had the courage to doubt, he would not have come to the place where he could say, "My Lord and my God!"

Among the deepest hurts of my life, believe it or not, was an intellectual one. I was searching for an answer to the dilemma of reconciling a God who is both good and all-powerful with the suffering of the innocent.

Every argument for God's side was lacking. If you blame suffering on the original sin of Adam, how do you explain God's making a creature who has the capacity to rebel and then holding Him accountable for doing it? Or worse still, how could a creature in perfect union with God choose to break the union and be called intelligent?

> **"If Thomas hadn't had the courage to doubt, he would not have come to the place where he could say, 'My Lord and my God!'"**

If you blame the devil for evil, you only remove the problem one step; you do not solve it. How could an angel in perfect union with God choose to be at enmity with Him, unless God had created him with the flaw for rebelling?

Even the argument I have been using in this book has holes in it. If our lives are for "soul-making," and pain is the means by which we grow toward the likeness of God, couldn't we grow with a little less pain?

I won't bore you with the rest of the classic arguments designed to explain how God can be good and powerful and allow evil all at the same time. Each was a dead-end street for me.

I was not only struggling with an innocent, handicapped child; I also could not find a way to hold my faith together intellectually. I had been in school for almost ten years past college. I was the pastor of a church expounding on the love of God each Sunday. And I did not even believe He existed. If you think it's hard to preach when you believe what you're saying—and it is—you should try preaching when you don't believe it.

I must admit that suicide was occasionally a considered option. "A man can endure any how as long as he has a why," said Nietzsche.[1] I understood him perfectly. As long as I had a structure which made sense—a why—I could face my troubles; as long as there was a "big picture," I could endure the how.

But when I lost the why, the how became intolerable. I would stay up all night reading, sleep just long enough for my fatigue level to subside, and then reawaken and read some more. There's more than one way to commit suicide.

One morning around three o'clock, I was reading a book called *God Beyond Doubt* (London: Oxford University Press, 1964) by a Scotsman named Geddes MacGregor. He talked about meeting God beyond "the skeptical fringe."

That phrase "the skeptical fringe" grabbed me. He said if you're going to start doubting the intellectual arguments for God, then don't stop doubting. Contest every claim. Reject every argument. Discard all morals and reason. In other words, go all the way with your doubting.

When you've done that, said MacGregor, then ask whether you want to live. If the answer is yes—that is, if you don't choose suicide—then ask *why* you want to live. What reasons are there for continuing your life? Why go on? Why keep rules? Why love? Why feel? Why be good?

I did as MacGregor suggested. In truth, I had already been doing it for months. Almost immediately I realized that if evil explains away God, I had a problem accounting for goodness. Where does it come from? "'The existence of goodness is a bigger problem for an atheist than the existence of evil is for a believer," said Harry Emerson Fosdick.[2]

Slowly it became clear to me that my doubting had in fact been bringing me to the greatest growth-leap of my life. I would never be able to solve the riddle of good-God-powerful-God versus evil. *What I had to do was make a choice to believe with the contradictions or to follow the implications of not believing to their logical conclusion.*

About that time I started reading the works of the Danish philosopher Søren Kierkegaard. I discovered that I was not the first pilgrim to reach this conclusion. His book *Either/Or*

(London: Oxford University Press, 1944) is about the same choice.

Either we choose to take the leap of faith *with the contradictions, or* we follow the trail of not believing to its logical end, which puts us in a world which is even more absurd.

So at 3:00 A.M. on the cold wintry plains of West Texas, I experienced my second conversion. There were no tears and trumpets this time. A quiet peace came upon me as I took the leap of faith and decided to believe along with the contradictions. I have never been afraid, intellectually, again.

I learned that the courage to doubt is the path to peace. I also learned that God will not allow Himself to be captured by our little logical systems.

"A perfectly logical God would be little more than a household pet. If we could explain Him, we would own Him."

In the Western world, knowledge is power. To know is to control. Therefore, a perfectly logical God would be little more than a household pet. If we could explain Him, we would own Him. God will not let us capture Him in our systems of thought. While we tinker with our logical boxes, He simply goes elsewhere.

I encourage you to bravely doubt.

COURAGEOUS IGNORANCE

Thomas had the courage to say, "I won't believe without some evidence." This courageous doubt had another facet to it that I call "courageous ignorance." He wasn't ashamed to say, "I don't know." He didn't let his pride keep him from asking after the truth.

In the John 14 passage which I noted earlier, *none* of Jesus' disciples knew what He meant when He said, "I go and prepare a place for you.... You know the way that leads to the place where I am going" (vv. 3-4). From their subsequent actions, they were clearly ignorant of His coming crucifixion.

Yet when He said, "You know where I'm going" they all must have nodded. All except Thomas. Only he had the courage to say, "No, we *don't* know where You're going. So how could we know the way?"

There's clout in doubt, especially if it is accompanied by the courage to admit that we don't know. I love Will Rogers's comment, "Everyone's ignorant, except on different subjects." Thomas knew that he didn't know.

While at an international religious conference, we were divided into small groups in which each person was invited to present a paper on his or her opinion of the future of religion in the twenty-first century. One brother from a European country presented his opinion in sonorous tones and scholarly language which lasted a full hour. When he had finished, the rest of us said, "Here! Here!" Then it was time for discussion and rebuttal.

Another European allowed as how he disagreed. A seminarian spoke up, proving that he had read a book. I was leaving on safari in two hours. Mentally and emotionally I was already sitting on the lawn of the Victoria Falls Hotel, listening to lions roar. To heck with the church in the twenty-first century!

A Russian Baptist leader interrupted the boring business. "I understand nothing in your paper," he said apologetically. "I am a simple man who is trying to share the hope of Jesus with my people. I know almost nothing of social trends and of the world beyond the walls of my city.

"This is the first time in my life that I have ever been outside of my own country," he continued. "I would like so much to tell my people of the faith of their Christian brothers in the free world. Could you tell me in simple words what Jesus means to you?"

We never got back to the paper. My mind came back from safari. These were the only words the Russian had uttered in two days. We didn't think he could speak English!

Each of us told our story of conversion. When it was the erudite brother's turn, he told a tender and beautiful story of being touched by God on a spring day by the seashore. His testimony was so foreign to the paper he had presented.

Then the Russian told an amazing story. He had been an officer in the KGB, assigned to harass "illegal worshipers." One night he and a fellow officer had rousted a small group of Christians who were meeting in a home. All escaped except one old woman. She appeared to be too feeble to run. However, the agents soon discovered that she had chosen to stay.

"God has told me not to run away from you," she said. "He has ordered me to tell you about Him."

"Come now, old grandmother," said the KGB agent, "why would you choose to defy your country and live out your days in prison because of a dead Jew?"

"I am not a traitor," she replied. "I stood with my husband at Leningrad against the Germans. When he fell, I took his place. I can still see his bright blood on the snow. I buried all of my children during the siege.

"Yes, I did this," she said, "and I was not afraid as I am not afraid now. God ordered me then as He orders me now. And the Jew is not dead. He lives!"

The Russian pastor and former KGB agent said, "Then she smiled at me and clasped my hand within hers. 'He is alive, you know, and you may know Him as well as I.'"

She was arrested, and he never saw her again, but he kept her New Testament and read it. "It is no surprise what happened to me then, ya?" he chuckled.

Had it not been for one courageously ignorant pastor's confession that he understood nothing of our bluster, we would have missed a rare moment. There's clout in doubt, especially if it's accompanied by a courage to say, "I don't know."

COURAGEOUS SURRENDER

The ultimate power of doubt is that it can lead us to the kind of surrender expressed in Thomas's words, "My Lord and my God!" Courageous doubt and courageous ignorance led to a determined willfulness, a decision to abandon old ways and start new ones.

Joy Davidman said, "all conversions are blessed defeats."[3] Thomas gave in, gave up, and gave over. Once he was grasped by the truth, he completely let go.

Of course, the immediate question is, "Who wouldn't?" If Jesus appeared to me and I could feel the nail prints and the gash, I'd believe, too! I'd have no other choice!

Jesus anticipated this reaction. That's why He responded to Thomas's pledge of allegiance by saying, "Do you believe because you see me? How happy are those who believe without seeing me!" (John 20:29).

On several occasions in this book I have mentioned the glimpses, tugs, and nudges I have received from God. I have said that without these rare and fleeting affirmations of God's presence, I could not believe. I stand by this statement. I suppose that's why I identify with Thomas. He had to have first-hand experience in order to believe.

But is this true for everybody? Must everyone have these indisputable encounters with a living God in order to transform trouble into triumph? I hope not. Because people frequently tell me they have never had such an experience.

Just last evening, I was visiting with my dear friends Wally and Rosie. God never made more gracious and generous people. I am using their lovely condominium by the sea as a retreat to write this book.

Wally was a pilot in World War II and served his country with distinction. He met Rosie during the war. They worked hard and honestly and were rewarded with America's bounty. They had a wonderful family and never forgot that God was the source of their blessings.

A few years ago their daughter, a mother of two, came home at midday to surprise two burglars who murdered her. One is now on death row; the other plea-bargained a sentence.

Through her tears last night, Rosie said, "I have heard you speak of those quiet and peaceful moments when God has become real to you in a personal way. If only He would do that for me! I try so hard to believe. I am told to forgive the animal who killed our daughter, but I cannot.

"I know he still owns and controls me as long as I hate him, but I still cannot forgive. Believe me, it would be wonderful to be rid of this bitterness, but every time I see how much my grandchildren need their mom and every time I think of how our system coddles mad-dogs and turns deaf ears to the cries of the blood of the innocent, I neither forgive nor forget."

"Maybe you're trying to be God." I just blurted it out. I don't know why I said it. "Only God can forgive something like that," I continued. "Perhaps you should simply surrender your hatred up to God. I don't mean let it go and detach yourself from it. You can't detach yourself. I mean put it on a platter and say, 'God, here it is! I can't do anything with it. You're going to have to love me, God, along with all of my bitterness. If I'm going to hell for hating this killer of my child, then I must go to hell. I cannot be You, God. I can only be me!'"

Then I told her of Corrie Ten Boom's post-war encounter with one of her former Gestapo prison guards.[4] Corrie was traveling throughout Europe after the war, preaching her message of forgiveness and healing. One night she exited the hall where she had just delivered her message, and she heard the voice of a man in front of her. "Ya," he said. "It is good that you teach forgiveness, Corrie Ten Boom. We must have that now and put the past behind us."

She knew the voice of this cruelest of the former concentration camp guards. He had regularly abused the inmates physically, sexually, and emotionally. Corrie's sister had died the day after he had made her stand naked in the cold and had abused her in front of the other inmates.

Corrie said a wave of rage swept over her. She could have killed him without the slightest remorse. She realized that these feelings were in contradiction with everything she had been preaching. Under her breath she said, "God forgive me. I cannot forgive this man." She had reached the limit of her power. All she could do was surrender herself, *along with the bitterness,* to God.

She said a peace swept over her that told her that her courageous surrender was enough. However, she did not succeed in ridding herself of her bitterness toward the monster of the concentration camp!

Rosie did not seem to be bowled over by my wonderful words. No peace swept over her. I promised to pray that she and Wally would find relief. And I do, every day.

But here's the point: Wally and Rosie go on believing *without seeing!* They have not abandoned their generosity. They have not with drawn into a shell and turned sour toward the world. They have not mounted up with wings as eagles, to be sure. Nor have they been able to run and not be weary. But they *have* continued to *walk and not faint,* and without any glimpses, tugs, and nudges!

I have come to believe that the glimpses, tugs, and nudges

may not be for the strongest persons in the kingdom. They may be for the weakest! God has given me these personal visitations because I *must* have them. "Do you believe because you have seen me?" says Jesus. "How blessed are those who believe without seeing me!"

If you are among the Wally and Rosie's of this world who have been cruelly abused by evil, I do not judge you. Frankly, your rage is not necessarily sick or sinful. True, the person you hate owns you, and your hatred can become all-consuming. You would be better off without it. It *is* true that if and when the "switch is pulled" on the perpetrator, there will be some closure to your agony. But the hurt and the anger will probably be with you for as long as you live. There are a few rare souls who are able to let it go. They are the ones who make the headlines and shame the rest of us.

As for us, all we can do is courageously surrender our bitterness up to God and ask Him to take us and it together. My prediction for those who make this courageous offering is that they will receive one of two things: Either a "Thomas experience," which enables them to say, "My Lord and my God" or the guts to get through, to walk and not faint, to build collaterals around the pebbles of evil which are lodged in their hearts.

AN ASIDE

I feel the need to speak to the matter of punishment—divine and criminal—somewhere in this book. Now is as good a time as any.

When it comes to the subject of criminal punishment within human society, I simply reconfirm what C. S. Lewis said over thirty years ago.[5] He foresaw the sorry state of affairs in which the criminal justice system now finds itself and believed it was because of a fundamental shift in the concept of the purpose of punishment which began in England and Europe around mid-century and has since spread to the U.S. Whereas punishment had been seen as "just dessert"—what the offender deserved for his crime—it came to be viewed as a means of cure and deterrence.

Once the purpose of punishment became deterrence and rehabilitation, the "experts"—psychiatrists, sociologists, criminologists—became the arbiters of the system. Formerly, when punishment was seen as deserved, i.e., as an earned reward, the courts represented the common people's view of morality and justice. The majority ethic governed criminal sentencing.

Now, the will of the common people has been exchanged for the will of the experts who, as Lewis so aptly points out, are only ordinary people themselves, except with extraordinary powers.

Society must have order. And that order must protect what the society at large deems valuable. Punishment should be the reward earned for breaching the order and safety of that society. Obviously, mercy must be built into the system, but the flaw of the current system is that it neither cures nor deters criminals, nor does it protect society.

My reason for discussing the subject here is simply to point out that a system which protects the victim and punishes the perpetrator is not inconsistent with a merciful, forgiving God. The kingdom of heaven and the kingdom of earth are two different realms. Jesus submitted Himself to the laws of the earth, even to capital punishment.

His statements on nonretaliation in the Sermon on the Mount have been used frequently as a scriptural basis for outlawing capital punishment. This is a distortion. The Sermon on the Mount was spoken to His disciples, not to the world in general. He was describing "life in the kingdom"—how they were to treat each other on a personal, everyday basis.

"To forgive is divine. But if you find that you are not God, then all you can do is offer up your bitterness honestly."

It is true that you cannot cure violence with violence. But it is also true that justice means rewarding behavior according to its contribution to the order of society.

Do not allow yourself to be intimidated by any prevailing "spirit of the age." There is clout in doubt.

I have chased a rabbit perhaps. I did it only because I wanted to speak to those of you who have been victimized by the senseless evil of people who seem to have lost all human sensitivity. Your sense of rage is altogether human, but it can also be altogether consuming.

You have every right to demand justice—which I define as the "dessert earned for behavior within society"—provided, of course, that you acknowledge your own need for mercy.

To forgive is divine. But if you find that you are not God, then all you can do is offer up your bitterness honestly. My prediction is that you will receive either a glimpse of God or the guts to get through.

11

It's Grateful
or Hateful

The great Texas drought of the 1950s put my dad down for the first time. He had retired at forty, sold his business, and purchased a three thousand-acre ranch in the Brazos delta, where Stephen F. Austin and the "Original 300" had settled Texas.

We had a big lake for fishing and duck hunting, rice fields, alligators, squirrels, quail, and deer. Dad poured all of his money into a hunting and fishing club and the cattle operation. He built a large house where he entertained hundreds of Texas's most notable and notorious.

As soon as all was in place, it stopped raining for almost four years. The lake couldn't be filled from the river. The bottom fell out of the cattle market. We couldn't water the rice. When I went off to college in the fall of 1956, we were still hanging on. If the rains would come in the spring, we could probably make it, Dad said.

The rains did come. Did they ever! Second only to Noah's flood! All of the reservoirs up and down the Brazos filled up completely, and still it kept raining. They had to open the dams.

I came home from school on a Friday afternoon. By night-fall the river was creeping into the bar ditches along the highway in front of the house. By midnight we were stacking furniture.

As dawn broke, our house was five feet under. Red Brazos silt oozed in and out of doors and windows. Velvet drapes soaked up the muddy goo. Chippendale furniture floated about the halls. Cattle were dead. The clubhouse and out-buildings of the hunting lodge were gone.

The final blow came when the river crested above its banks and got into the lake. Soon the levies broke, sweeping away everything that was left.

Dad and Mom and brother and little sister and I piled what we could save onto two skiffs and began to wade to high ground a mile away. Mom had salvaged her china, silver, and some paintings valued at almost one hundred thousand dollars.

As we approached the highway, which was under water, some sightseers came rushing by in a motorboat. The wake tipped over the skiff with Mom's stuff in it. The sightseers looked back in time to see Dad reaching for his shotgun. They didn't stop to help.

The capsizing of the boat full of valuables was symbolic. All that Mom and Dad had worked for since they had married at sixteen with nothing except their clothes had literally been overturned and sunk in the mud.

Mom began to sob. Dad began to sing. The only song he knew was "There's No Place Like Home." The more he sang, the more Mama cried. We children didn't know whether we should sing with Daddy or wail with Mama. We thought they had both gone mad.

Daddy was a "Texas Cusser," a Texan who's made profanity such a part of his regular vocabulary that he doesn't mean anything by it, and in fact does not sound all that profane when he uses it.

Mama's wailing finally drowned out Daddy's singing, so he started yelling. (I shall clean up what he said, even though the story loses something when I do. You're welcome to use your imagination. If you've heard George Carlin's routine on "stuff" it will help.)

"Doggone it, woman!" he shouted. "All we've lost is *stuff!* When we married, we didn't have no *stuff!* Nor a pot to hold it!! All we had was our clothes and a quarter, which I gave to the preacher. Then we got all of this *stuff.* We got so much *stuff* that we had to build a bigger barn to put it in.

"Now we ain't got no more *stuff!* But, h- - -, woman, we can always get some more stuff! I can't wait to give what's left back to them steely-eyed bankers so we can go get some more stuff! We got everything we need right here. We got our family and our wits."

Mama wouldn't be consoled, but Daddy wouldn't be denied. He took her by both shoulders and looked her straight in the eye. "It's just stuff, Mama," he said. "And I'm gladder that I had it than madder that I lost it!"

"God is really not interested in your money. The preacher definitely is!"

They lost the club, the ranch, everything, but every creditor was paid in full. When all accounts were settled, they were back where they had started years before. Ten years later they had more "stuff" than before, and Dad had the same healthy disrespect for it.

The "stuff story" has helped many people over the years. Whenever I tell it, I get letters from all over the country. People like it because it illustrates the biblical attitude toward everything we call "ours"—our material possessions, our toys, our family members, our ideas, our achievements.

As the Bible sees it, there are only two possible postures we can take toward anything called ours. *We can be grateful, or we can be "hateful."*

In the first chapter of Paul's letter to the Romans, he says the wrath of God is brought to bear against people who hate the truth (Romans 1:18). The word *to hate* means to stifle, to prevent from being exposed.

Then Paul goes on to define "hating the truth." He says all humans look at the created order and know in their hearts that there is a "Creative Source" behind it. Yet, our universal flaw is that we do not honor this Source by being *grateful!* (Romans 1:21).

To be hateful simply means to be ungrateful, to look at all we have and to feel no sense of indebtedness for it.

Lofton Hudson wrote a book entitled, *Grace Is Not a Blue-Eyed Blond.* He pointed out that Jesus' view of sin was quite different from what we're apt to hear today.[1] Jesus didn't define sin. Instead He gave some short-subject movies of people in the act of sinning.

Several of these short subjects portray people who have no sense of being in debt for what they enjoy. There's a farmer who has a bumper crop and decides that he's bulletproof for life. He stores it up and sits back and denies any obligation to share (Luke 12:13ff.).

There's a young man who demands his inheritance from his father. He uses the words *I, my,* and *mine.* He has no sense of gratitude (Luke 15: 11ff.).

A Pharisee finds himself praying in the temple beside a tax collector and says to God, "How proud I am not to be like this lowly sinner! I pray, tithe, study..." (Luke 18:9ff.). He thinks his status in life is deserved and earned. He has no sense of it being given to him as a gracious gift.

We either live gratefully or we live hatefully toward all that is. We are either a plus in the stream of life, or we are a minus.

I tell my people during our attempts to raise money to finance the mission of our church that giving money needs to be set within a larger context. God is really not interested in your money. The preacher definitely is! But God is not. God is interested in how you look at the whole of life on this earth. Either you are putting something back into the stream of life, or you are living off of it.

The idea of tithing, giving 10 percent of all that comes into our hands back to God, originated when God's people stopped being nomads and became farmers. When they harvested their first crop and began to consume it, they realized they needed to save back some seed to replant, or they would die.

That is true of the whole of life. You either put something back, or you eat it all up. My point here is that *the decision to put something back is grounded in gratitude, while the decision to consume without giving back is a rejection of life itself.* To horde your "stuff," your ideas, your talent, your love is to hate life itself. To see these things as undeserved gifts and to put something back into the stream of life is to be part of the solution.

LOSS

Nowhere is gratitude more essential than in dealing with life's losses, whether they be material, emotional, or spiritual.

"I'm gladder that I had it than madder that I lost it," is the breakfast of champions when it comes to suffering. Dad, with his sixth-grade education, had learned a wise truth about standing up to tragedy. He focused on being grateful for having had it at all, instead of being hateful for having lost it.

Earlier, I mentioned John Claypool's sermons which he

delivered during and following his twelve-year-old daughter's fatal battle with leukemia.[2] In the first sermon he delivered to his congregation after her death, he told the people how they could help him best.

He did not need answers explaining why Laura Lue had died. He had already heard those from well-meaning friends. Besides, Carlyle Marney had given him the only answer that made the slightest sense: Someday God has a lot of explaining to do.

Nor did he need to hear that time would heal his hurts. It surely would not, but even if it did, he was hurting now.

He didn't need to hear of how others had gone through the same kind of experience either. Oh, it was good to know that others knew what he was feeling, but when you're where he was, sharing "war stories" is of little benefit. How many times have you heard someone trying to comfort the bereaved by saying, "I remember when I lost my Henry"? Hurting people don't really care to hear about "your Henry!" They're just trying to survive.

Claypool told his people they could help him by reminding him regularly that all of life, especially the life of his child, is a gift not to be taken for granted *or for our own.* Laura Lue had never been *his.* She was only *on loan* from God. And the only way he could make it through the pain was to be grateful for having had her for a while, rather than being hateful for having lost her. In short, he was gladder that he had her than madder that he had lost her.

When people call me on my TV program and pour out their grief, I always do two things. First, I try to get them to realize that all grief is loss and to identify what they have lost. Then I ask them if they would rather have had it and lost it or never had it at all.

For example, one night during a commercial break, the director rushed onto the set and said, "There's an elderly sounding gentleman on the line. He's sobbing. His dog has died. He's completely alone. He wants to talk to you *on the air!* What shall we do?"

"Put him on," I said. My mind raced for the thirty seconds that I had before we went live again. *Why had I agreed to take the call? I mean, a dead dog for heaven's sake! Was I out of my mind?*

I knew I had taken the call because there was a hurting old man out there in the night whose last intimate contact with anything living had been lost. There was nothing between him and the void but a telephone, a TV, and a preacher who appeared to care.

He didn't say three words before he broke down. "I know it must sound silly to you and your listeners, but I just had to talk to someone."

"Who cares whether it sounds silly?" I said. "Tell me exactly what you're feeling."

"Like crap!" he said on national TV. Ask a silly nondirective question, get a real answer!

"I mean, tell me if you've ever felt this way before."

"Oh, yes," he sobbed. "It's the same as when our little boy died in the Korean War and when my wife died three years ago."

"Have there been other times when you've felt this way?" I asked.

"Come to think of it—and, boy, this *is* silly—I felt this when my first girlfriend jilted me."

The point is obvious. I was getting him to define his losses, one at a time, and how each felt.

Then I asked him the second question. "Would you rather have had your dog, your son, your wife, and your girlfriend and lost them, or never have had them at all?"

"Right now, I wish I'd never had them at all," he answered. "All life has ever done for me is set me up for one crushing loss after another."

I was stunned. I tried to recover. This was live television, and I had manipulated this man into giving me the answer I wanted, but he had given me the wrong answer!

"Well," I stuttered, "let me ask you to do something for me. When you hang up the phone, get a piece of paper and write down the names of all of the loves you've lost. Under each name, write down every joyful, fun time you can remember having with them. Then answer the question I've asked you again."

"I don't need to do that," he said. "I know that I will decide it was better to have had and lost than not to have had at all. But I'm just hurting so bad right now that I don't want to be grateful."

I do not know of another pathway through the thicket of suffering than the pathway of gratitude. If we cannot see that everything we've had was really a gift on loan and be grateful for the loan of it, we shall remain bitter.

"If we cannot see that everything we've had was really a gift on loan and be grateful for the loan of it, we shall remain bitter."

BETRAYAL

The hurt which comes from betrayal also presents us with the "hateful or grateful" dilemma. When someone you love lets you down, you are faced with the decision of whether to risk loving again or to go into your shell. Almost all dysfunctional relationships can be traced back to betrayal, real or imagined.

I started receiving threatening telephone calls soon after beginning a local daily television talk show in our town. A young woman would call late at night. When she knew I was on the line, she would let go with a string of filthy epithets that sounded as if they came from those movie versions of the demon-possessed. Then she would tell me I was going to die and hang up.

I called the telephone company and the authorities, but they said they couldn't help. (This is no longer the case, by the way.) I changed phone numbers. She found me again. I had my number unlisted. Still she found me.

After two years of this harassment, I brought it to an end. She called about 3:00 A.M. As soon as she began her diatribe, I quietly said, "Operator, tape this call." She hung up immediately.

In two minutes she called back, crying. "Please don't send me to jail, Dr. Mann," she pleaded.

"You wanna talk?" I said kindly.

We talked till daylight. She was a young mother of two, married to a truck driver who was gone most nights. Her father had died when she was six, and her family had been split up and scattered across the country.

"I have done this to preachers in every town where we've lived for years," she said.

"Why preachers?" I asked.

"When my father was very ill, a preacher came to our house and laid hands on him to heal him," she said. "When the preacher got ready to leave, I asked him if my daddy was going to die. He said, no, Daddy wouldn't die because he had been filled with the Holy Spirit. Well, Daddy did die! The preacher came back to the house with several members of the church. They circled the bed where Daddy lay. One by one they spoke in an unknown tongue and ranted and raved. The preacher said if they believed hard enough, then they could raise Daddy from the dead. Well, they didn't and they couldn't."

After a moment of complete silence, she said, "I've hated preachers ever since. They're traitors." This tortured soul had been torturing others because of what she considered betrayal.

The attitude of gratitude I've been describing is good medicine for healing the betrayed. The Old Testament hero, Joseph, is a grand example of the power of choosing to be grateful instead of hateful in the face of betrayal.

Joseph was the beloved son of Jacob and his favorite wife Rachel. Jacob had ten sons by Rachel's sister, Leah, whom he had to marry first in order to get Rachel. To make matters worse, Rachel was barren, a condition of which she was frequently reminded by Leah.

Finally, Rachel gave birth to Joseph, and he was the apple of Jacob's eye. He didn't have to work in the fields like his older brothers. He had a coat of bright colors, which signified his favored status with his father.

As he approached his teen years, he began to "rub it in" with his brothers. One day he found them working in the countryside and re minded them that one day they would all be working for him. They turned on him. First they threw him into a pit and left him to die. Then they relented and sold him into slavery to a caravan bound for Egypt. From a prince to a slave in one day! And at the hands of his own brothers! Betrayal!

In Egypt he was sold to one of the Pharaoh's chief commanders named Potiphar. His ingenuity and intelligence quickly led him to the management of Potiphar's entire household staff and the affections of Potiphar's wife. She made a pass at him. He rejected her. She told Potiphar it was Joseph who had made the advances. So Joseph went to prison. Betrayal!

While in prison, Joseph fell in with two of Pharaoh's staff who were momentarily out of favor. When Joseph showed a talent for interpreting their dreams, they promised to bring the injustice of Joseph's imprisonment to Pharaoh's attention. One was released and restored, as Joseph had predicted, but he quickly forgot his promise. Betrayal!

Later, as you know, Joseph rose to become second only to Pharaoh. Because of his foresight in storing grain during the years of plenty, he saved Egypt from famine. In fact, it was this pre-planned prosperity which brought Joseph's long-lost brothers to Egypt in search of grain.

The touching story of their reunion with Joseph stands as a monument to the way gratitude can help us overcome the hurt of betrayal. Joseph gives the brothers grain and sends them to fetch his father and family to Egypt. But his brothers are afraid that Joseph will exact his vengeance for their betrayal. When they come begging for his mercy, he breaks down and weeps. "Don't be afraid; I can't put myself in the place of God. You plotted evil against me, but God turned it into good, in order to preserve the lives of many people.... You have nothing to fear" (Genesis 50:19-21).

Those few sentences tell volumes about how Joseph used "the grateful" instead of "the hateful" in dealing with betrayal.

First, he had a knack for getting inside the skin of others, feeling what they felt. No doubt he lay awake many nights replaying how he had strutted about lording it over his brothers who, through no choice of their own, had been dealt a bad hand. He must have been grateful that, given the circumstances, he still had his life and his wits.

He must have understood that Potiphar's wife was from a different moral setting and perhaps lonely and neglected. He had known rejection, so he knew how she felt when she was rejected. And again he was grateful that he still had his life and his wits.

In spite of all the doting and spoiling he received from his parents, Joseph did have a strong sense that he had been born as part of a grander scheme laid out by God. Joseph did not believe in accidents. Instead of fretting when life tumbled in, he asked, "What is God up to now?" Instead of cursing what lay ahead, he said, "Won't it be interesting to see how this turns out?"

In every tragedy you can look at what you've lost and be hateful, or you can look at what you have left and be grateful. After each betrayal, Joseph focused on what was left and gave thanks.

MY LIFE

The "grateful or hateful" principle can be applied to something else we think we own, namely our own lives. We can look at the thing called "me"—that bundle of living which is contained in what we call "the self"—as a gift on loan or as ours to do with as we please.

The Bible says, "You are not your own." Have you ever thought through that sentence? Two "you's" are mentioned in it, two selves. "*I* don't own *me*."

Jesus said on several occasions, "If you hold on to your life, you'll lose it. If you let go of your life, you'll keep it eternally." Two selves again!

I think these statements are telling us that our lives are only ours to manage. We can be hateful toward them by refusing to give them away, or we can be grateful toward them and see them as gifts and use them as gifts for giving to others.

I know all of this is high sounding, especially in a society which has been obsessed with demanding *my* rights, *my* space, *my* face, and *my* place for many years.

Nevertheless, there are only two possible postures toward your own life: grateful or hateful. To be grateful toward yourself is to be free to give yourself. Liberty is the freedom to give gratefully the self I have received from God. Independence,

which is a thief in liberty's clothing, is the self-destructive tendency to refuse to grow and care.

I cannot think of a better way to hate one's own life than to decide not to share it. To declare that I am free to do as I please as long as I hurt no one else is to declare that I can exist without relationships. I declare that I am not human.

Some years back, William Raspberry, the gifted columnist for the *Washington Post,* wrote about a social ill in America. His column pointed to the odd fact that newly arrived Asian immigrants to the U.S. were flourishing economically and socially, while, proportionately speaking, the majority of black Americans were not, although they had been here for much longer.

Raspberry concluded that the reason was mostly because of self-image and worldview. The Vietnamese, Cambodians, etc., saw themselves as finally unfettered by oppressive forces over which they had no control. They had been set free to become

---

"Liberty is the freedom to give gratefully the self I have received from God. Independence, which is a thief in liberty's clothing, is the self-destructive tendency to refuse to grow and care."

---

and pursue their own potential. They saw the American society as a candy store without bars. "Just let me in there!" was their dominant feeling. The result was and is that the Asians have flourished, some even in the midst of the very ghettos which are supposed to be social prisons for the ambitious.

Many black Americans, on the other hand, began with a different self-image, said Raspberry. They saw themselves as isolated, oppressed, and different from others. Their focus was on their separateness and, in some cases, perceived wretchedness.

Their worldview was that the candy store had bars on it. The result was and is that many blacks can only curse the system and rebel in hopelessness.[3]

This is self-hatred par excellence. When I see my life as my own, *even if I am forced to by my social conditions,* I am my own worst enemy. But if I can look at me as a gift on loan to use and multiply and share, then I can grow through the worst of conditions.

Someone has said, there are only two kinds of people: those who are out to make a better place for themselves in the world and those who are out to make the world a better place for everybody. It's grateful or hateful.

12

Choose To Lose

There's a legend about a serious young priest who is afraid that he cannot attain the level of devotion that God requires.[1] He confesses and fasts and does penance daily. He takes contemplative retreats and lives among the sick and poor.

Still there is no relief from the guilt which torments his soul. Eventually, he makes a pilgrimage to a remote island where the saints of God are said to dwell. These are the ones who have ceased all wanting and renounced all pleasure, save the joy of total concentration on God.

The young priest searches out the eldest and wisest of the holy hermits. "Father," he asks, "do you still wrestle with the devil as I do?"

"Oh, no, my son. I am beyond such nonsense now. The devil is only a poor excuse for feeding one's own desires."

"Well, then," says the seeker, "I suppose you wrestle with the darkness within your own soul?"

"No," says the hermit, "I now only wrestle with God."

"You wrestle with God! But do you hope to win?"

"Oh, no, my son, I hope to lose."

Throughout this book I have been describing techniques which arouse the fighting spirit within us, the guts to get

through, the stamina to stand up and take it. *But there are some battles we need to lose in order to win the war over our suffering.*

I agree with the hermit that our real battle is not against the devil. Don't get me wrong; the devil is real. Evil is greater than the sum of its parts, and if we give in to the dark forces within ourselves, we lose the power to choose the good.

All you have to do in order to believe in the overwhelming presence of evil among humankind is read the morning paper. Or better still, get honest with yourself. There is within us all a universal blood lust, an overpowering self-interest, a will to power and control.

I recognized this tendency within myself during the Mideast War of 1991. I was against our getting into it, but once we were committed, I found myself glued to the "war show" on television. With every allied victory, I applauded.

Publicly, I maintained a circumspect façade, but inwardly I was thrilled at how well we were doing. And when I heard that over one hundred thousand Iraqis were annihilated, I did what victors often do. I blamed their deaths on them!

The devil is alive and well, but we give him far too much credit. C. S. Lewis was right; there are two *equally* great errors in our attitude toward the devil. One is to take him too lightly, and the other is to take him too seriously.[2]

As I said, I agree with the hermit. Our war is mainly with God.

All human evil stems from two great battles we fight with God. The rest of our struggles are merely skirmishes. Unless we make a willful choice to lose these two, we cannot "make our souls," we cannot transform trouble into triumph.

THE BATTLE TO CUT GOD DOWN TO MY SIZE

I want a manageable God, one who will endorse all of the myths of superiority that I have invented and which have been

passed down to me by my ancestors. When I play the "what-would-Jesus-do-if-He-came-back-today" game, I always tend to imagine Him doing what I like, saying what I like, and attacking those I don't like.

I don't think I am alone in this. Only a few months ago, I went to hear Matthew Fox, guru and pioneer of New Age thinking. I admire anyone who is trying to lead us beyond the narrow prejudices of our race, creed, and nation. I think we must all begin to think "beyond the boundaries" which separate us. So I went to hear Fox. At one point in his well-received speech, he gave the opinion that if the founders of the world's major religions were to return to earth in present times,

> **"C. S. Lewis was right; there are two equally great errors in our attitude toward the devil. One is to take him too lightly, and the other is to take him too seriously."**

they wouldn't join the movements they birthed. In other words, Buddha wouldn't be a Buddhist, Mohammed wouldn't be a Muslim, and Jesus wouldn't be a Christian. That sounded "right" to me at first glance. But then I realized that Fox was doing exactly what we have been doing forever. We figure out what we think the "true faith" is, and then we project our prejudices onto Jesus, or whomever. Fox was really saying, "If Jesus came back today, He would agree with me!"

Dorothy Sayers said, "We have efficiently pared the claws of the Lion of Judah, certified Him meek and mild, and made Him a fitting household pet for pale curates and pious old ladies."[3] We all want to whittle God down to our size.

Carlyle Marney's book *Priests to Each Other* is among the five books which have influenced me most in my religious formation. He says we project images of ourselves onto God and then worship the images![4] God is a white Anglo-Saxon Protestant, or He is a black social reformer. I heard of a zealous young coed who said, "Well, even if Jesus was a Jew, God's still a Baptist!"

You can cut God down to the size of your particular interpretation of Scripture. I did it for years. During my traveling revival days, I had the same attitude toward preaching that my teenagers have toward their stereo systems—nothing was worth hearing unless it was turned up loud. I confined God to my simplistic, guilt-inducing interpretation of the Bible. The *interpretation* became God; the Bible was God. I was a preacher of the Bible; therefore, I was God speaking.

An idol is anything you use to confine God to one place, one scheme, one man-made box. The reason the ancient Hebrews kept getting into trouble was that they kept trying to *localize* God within their own things.

You can cut God down to your reasoning ability. To say God cannot operate outside of my ability to comprehend Him is the same as saying He cannot operate outside of my interpretation of the Bible.

I have said in all of my previous books that religious liberals and conservatives are really brothers under the skin. They have both robbed God of His mystery. They have whittled and fitted God into their systems. That's why they spend so much time calling each other names.

When the serpent appears to the first couple in the Garden, the temptation is that Adam and Eve will be able to bring God down to their level by disobeying Him. "You will not die," says the snake. "God said that because he knows that when you eat [the fruit] you will be like God" (Genesis 3:4-5). "To know as God knows" is the temptation of every Adam and every Eve. We all want to reduce God to our comprehension.

The result is always the same. We can't live in the Garden anymore because our relationships are broken. Trust is broken down—*our* trust in God, not His in us.

We must choose to lose the struggle to cut God down to our size in order to win the wars of life. But this is especially true when it comes to our war with pain and suffering.

I have already said numerous times that the quest to understand why "bad things happen to good people" is a dead-end pursuit. Whether you are seeking logical or moral reconciliation, you cannot reconcile a good and powerful God with the suffering of the innocent. The suffering of the innocent is illogical and immoral from our perspective.

Now I want to add another statement which may sound just as harsh: If we could explain suffering logically and morally, we would *be God!* The hard truth is that we are *not.* Isn't this what Job finally ran up against? He was a good man by all criteria, yet he lost his family, his fortune, his health, and his friends. Over and over again, he demands to know why. God accepts his complaints and his anger and his bitterness and even his plea to die.

But God never allows Himself to be cut down to Job's size. He gives no logical and moral explanation. On the contrary, God says, "Who are you to question my wisdom with your ignorant, empty words? Stand up now like a man and answer me! Were you there when I made the world?" (Job 38:1-4).

The point is that Job must choose to lose in his effort to reduce God to his reason and morality. And Job does. Consequently, his surrender in the midst of suffering takes him to the place where he can *serve God for nothing.*

"Religious liberals and conservatives are really brothers under the skin. They have both robbed God of His mystery."

Job's entire tragedy is set within the context of a question: "Will a man serve God for nothing?" (Job 1:9). Job has everything—wealth, health, and family. Who wouldn't believe in God in those circumstances? But will Job still serve God if everything is taken away—*everything, including the logical and moral explanations for his suffering?* Job wins the war of suffering by choosing to lose the battle of understanding.

I was the pastor of a remarkable woman called Tiny. Her husband had died after a long bout with cancer. In mid-life, she was left with three children, a boy and twin girls.

Tiny worked three jobs. Her son handled grief by being absent most of the time. One of the twins lost her sight from a congenital disease. Then the other, who was the light of her life, contracted terminal leukemia.

The church rallied regularly to help as they could. I was so intimidated by Tiny's strength and calm that I always felt uncomfortable in her presence. I didn't know what to say. I couldn't fathom why she didn't disintegrate. Whenever she came to worship, I would lose my place in my sermons.

One day I asked if I might see her. I went to the rented house where she lived. We fumbled through iced tea and cookies and idle chat.

Finally I said, "Tiny, your suffering perplexes me like none I have ever experienced. You have such a calm determination about you. You don't cry in public. You don't transfer your anger onto others. You've never even asked to talk to me. You just go along like you haven't a problem in this world.

"I know the signs of grief, believe me," I said. "Yet I don't detect them in you."

By this time my voice was cracking, and I was almost in tears. She reached over and patted me on the knee. "I'm sorry that my responses to my situation threaten you," she said. "I know you want to help minister to me. Really, you want to fix me, but I seem so broken that you don't know where to start. Right?

"Well, I'm going to tell you how I get through. It will sound strange, but here it is. Long ago I decided that either I could go mad trying to understand my suffering, or I could draw upon the power that faith in God could save me.

"To tell you the truth, I do not know if God even exists. He may very well be a creation of my mind to keep me sane. All I can tell you is that I choose to believe and walk as the Bible tells me I should. I may be dreaming, but I'd rather live in the dream world of faith than in the nightmare of having to understand and justify God."

To transform trouble we must choose to lose the battle to cut God down to our size. The potter never explains himself to the clay, as God reminded Jeremiah.

You can question God. Personal relationships are built on dialogue, not monologue. You can vent your anger toward God as well. But this can become an addictive means of trying to become God. Physiological research has shown that whenever we vent rage, we get an endorphin rush like the kind of high that runners get or that we get when our favorite team wins a game.

We can pervert honest questioning and authentic anger which come from suffering, into an addictive attempt to "become as God." To win the war of woe, we must choose to lose the battle of forcing God into our airtight explanations. Tiny realized this.

THE BATTLE TO KEEP GOD FROM GROWING ME UP TO HIS SIZE

The second great conflict we must choose to lose is the flip side of the first—the battle to resist God's efforts to raise us to a higher level of humanity. If the first battle is to *humanize God,* the second is to *animalize ourselves.* On the one side, we want to bring God down to our level. On the other side, we don't want to be lifted up toward His.

We have been conditioned to abhor the mere mention of humans having the capacity to become like God. But the fact is that God *does* intend for us all to enjoy His kind of existence. Jesus was sent to show us what God has in mind for all of us. He called Himself Son of Man, as well as Son of God. Jesus is indeed the name of our species. He is what we are all coming to eventually. He Himself said, "But as many as received Him, to them He gave the right to become children of God" (John 1:12).

"I almost got fired one time
for suggesting that Jesus was more human
than we think and that we can be more
divine than we think."

We face the desire to take the course of least resistance, the easy way, every day of our lives, and it is as strong within us as the desire to play God. The will to inertia is as strong as the will to power.

In fact, it may be stronger! The overwhelming majority of humankind is content to wallow along in mediocrity, never thinking a new thought, never dreaming a new dream.

I come up with a book idea every week. I've been creating book titles for twenty years, yet this is only my fourth book. Why? Because I would rather conceptualize than actualize. I tell myself that simply conceiving the idea is the equivalent of actually writing it.

Telling a lie is easier than telling the truth. Complaining about Congress is easier than running for Congress. It is easier to fight or take flight than to make peace. Someone has said, "All it takes for evil to triumph is for good men to do nothing."

Almost all of the sermons I've heard on the subject of sin

deal with our attempts to be like God. I've heard very few about our *refusal* to become like God. Is that because more of us are guilty of the latter than the former?

I almost got fired one time for suggesting that Jesus was more human than we think and that we can be more divine than we think. I started by asking the question: Why is it that we use only a fraction of our mental powers throughout our lives? Most humans use only about 5 percent of their potential brain power. Geniuses use only about 10 per cent. We have this vast reservoir of untapped wasted energy.

I began to muse about what would happen if we had full use of the reservoir. We know, for example, that the mind has a profound effect on the body during illness. Isn't it plausible that with "full access" we could detect and reverse disease in our own bodies and in the bodies of others?

Matter is energy, I said. Material objects are only different aggregates of energy. If we had "full access," isn't it conceivable that we could decompose, teleport, and recompose?

Mouths were agape by now. The physicists in my congregation were laughing. The biblicists were grinding their teeth. But I pressed on.

"What if Jesus were a man who had full access to His potential—physically, mentally, and spiritually?" I asked. "Maybe He could do things which any human with such access could do. Maybe He would heal diseases with touch and walk on water and through closed doors! And maybe the result of sin is the shutting off of our access to our potential."

I stopped there. I've never heard so many so quiet.

"The reason you don't like this," I said, "is because you think it cheapens the image of our Lord."

"Amen!" they said.

"And you don't want Jesus' works to be explained in some weird way."

"Amen!" they said.

"And you think it's heresy to suggest that we ourselves might find the capacity to do what He did, right?"

"Amen!"

We call such thought heresy because we are part of a larger heresy. *We do not want Jesus to be human, because the more human He is, the more divine we are called to be.*

Scott Peck says we make Jesus 99.5 percent divine and 0.5 percent human. "Because the gulf is so great, American Christians are not seriously encouraged to bridge it. When Jesus said all those things about being the way... and that we were to be like Him and might even do greater things than He did, He couldn't possibly have been serious, could He?... it is through the large-scale ignoring of Jesus' real humanity that we are allowed to worship Him in name without the obligation of following in His footsteps."[5]

So it is just as destructive to keep God from raising us up to His level as it is to cut Him down to ours. We must choose to lose this second battle as well, if we are to metabolize our suffering.

At no time are we called upon more to reach above our ordinary humanity than when we are stricken with suffering.

When Elizabeth Kübler-Ross visited our church, she said that evil always presents us with the "high choice" or the "low choice." To illustrate the high choice, she told of a mother who was on a weekend trip to the California seaside with several of her friends who had children the same age as hers.

One morning the moms were sitting on a pier watching their small children paddle about in the surf. All of the children had on life vests, and the lifeguard was nearby.

Suddenly the water around the children boiled. A huge shark took the mother's child. Nothing was left but pieces of the life vest and frothy crimson water.

Kübler-Ross was summoned about two months later. She found the mother in a catatonic state. For almost a year,

Kübler-Ross led her back from the brink. "That was ten years ago," said Kübler-Ross. "Today the mother directs a program to help the parents of over ten thousand children who have died violently. She made the high choice."

How could someone make such a choice? There is only one explanation. She did not refuse to allow God to raise her to her higher potential. She didn't give in to the temptation to be "merely human." She allowed God to raise her up a notch.

Not long ago I felt betrayed by a fellow minister. I no longer feel this way, but I certainly felt that way then, and I felt that I had good cause. I had hired him when he was struggling to finish school, asked the church to pay him a fine salary and allow him to continue his education. I even got our church to pay his plane fare for commuting and one of our automobile dealers to furnish him a free car.

He was extremely talented. In a couple of years, he led a sizable group within the church. One Sunday morning without letting me know fully of his plans, he announced that he and the group were leaving to form an "authentic New Testament church" in our city. He gave two weeks' notice.

After he made his announcement at the first service, I had to close it with some kind of impromptu response! I wished him Godspeed and blessings. Inwardly, I was stunned.

The next service was only thirty minutes away. By the time it began, everyone knew the scuttlebutt. I had to preach and hear him give his swan song again. I blessed and affirmed him again. By now, I was angry, but I kept my cool.

Now I had to deal with his announcement that he would be there one more Sunday. I went into the sorry-for-myself syndrome. Not only had he eaten at my table and stolen my sheep, he was now going to stay over and rub it in for one more week.

I met with the church council and got no relief. They actually told me to take off the next Sunday if I couldn't keep my cool. I felt abandoned. I wallowed in self-pity. I told myself: "On top of all the other hurts, my own closest friends have chosen to let me suffer further indignity rather than giving the traitor a day off!"

In my mind I resigned and withdrew the resignation three times before the next Sunday. The only reason I withdrew it was in order to choose my own time to leave. There was no question in my mind that I *would* leave; it was simply a matter of when.

The "street kid" in me said, "Choose your own time; don't let others choose it for you." My world had fallen in. I felt that the great church I had been born to build was gone.

I couldn't prepare a sermon for the coming Sunday. I tried, but no message came. All I could do was envision what it would be like sharing the platform with "the traitor."

By Saturday, I had come to my senses somewhat. I would not allow my lower nature to rule my behavior. I prepared a sermon and planned to "keep my place in line."

Sunday morning it was ten degrees and sleeting. The entire city was shut down, and all roads were closed. God, or somebody, froze us out.

Monday was no better. I was shut away from the world for two days. I spent it taking inventory—of my life and, afterward, of my old sermon files.

I pulled out some notes from 1960. I had been to hear a preacher whom I admired greatly. He had talked about Paul writing to Timothy from prison. All of his friends had abandoned him—Demas, Crescens, Titus, Alexander the metal worker. "No one stood by me, when I defended myself," said Paul (2 Timothy 4:16). "All deserted me. But the Lord stayed with me and gave me strength . . . and he will rescue me from all evil" (2 Timothy 4:18).

At the bottom of my notes, I had written a poem. I was an idealistic believer of twenty-two, given to writing crude sentimentalities.

> Lord, I'm a raindrop, make me a sea;
> Lord, I'm an acorn, make me a tree.
> Lord, I'm a pebble, make me a mountain;
> Lord, I'm a trickle, make me a fountain.
> Lord, I'm one voice, make me a choir;
> Lord, I'm a spark, make me a fire.

The message to me from God was clear. I had a choice—I could choose to lose the battle to keep Him from growing me up to His size, or I could wallow in self-pity.

That was over two years ago. The church fellowship is healthier than ever. The group which left is fulfilling its mission, and I have made peace with their leader. My council was right, and I was wrong.

There are three requirements for church leaders: (1) They must be committed to Christ's mission for the church. (2) They must lead by serving. (3) They must support the pastor by not letting him own them. My council met all three criteria.

Thank God, they reminded me that there are battles I must choose to lose: the battle to cut God down to my size and the battle to keep Him from raising me up to His. There's no transforming trouble into triumph till you choose to lose them both.

13

It's What Happens to What Happens to You

I went through six commencement exercises from age eleven to thirty. I did not escape one without having to listen to William Ernest Henley's, "It matters not how straight the gate, how charged with punishments the scroll. I am the master of my fate; I am the captain of my soul."[1] Nor did I escape being told that I and my frightened classmates could change the world. We were always on the *brink* of something, either great disaster or great opportunity. Never did I graduate at an ordinary time in history. If I mastered my fate and captained my soul according to the great principles of my American forefathers, I could determine what happened to me and others around me.

I wish just one of those commencement speakers had told the story of Sir Reginald T. Atwater and the royal yacht *Britannia*. One evening the royal yacht was sailing with the Queen and her guests. At the helm was Sir Reginald T. Atwater who had captained the yacht without mishap for thirty-six years. All of a sudden he saw lights approaching dead ahead. He tried raising the approaching vessel by radio. No answer. So he went to his signal light and started flashing in Morse code. "This is the royal yacht *Britannia.* Give way immediately."

The message flashed back, "Cannot give way."

Atwater was stunned. He flashed his reply: "This is Her Majesty's vessel, and I have royal personages aboard. We alter course for no one. I am Captain Sir Reginald T. Atwater, and I have been the master of this ship for thirty-six years. I am ordering you to move out of the bloody way!"

There was a long pause. Then the message came blinking back: "This is bosun's mate Billy Bob Peake here. And I have been the keeper of this bloody lighthouse for two years..."

Sometimes we must change course no matter who we are. I am not, in fact, the master of my fate, and when it comes to my soul, I am not even a bosun's mate, let alone a captain.

Freedom does not mean that we can determine what happens to us or our world. You have no control over when you were born or where, your I.Q., genetic makeup, color, economic stratum, or susceptibility to disease.

What does freedom mean? It means that you are free to determine *what happens to what happens* to you. You can only respond to the givens of your life. You cannot move lighthouses; you must steer around them.

Viktor Frankl wrote a little book entitled *Man's Search for Meaning* that contains the basic precepts of his revolutionary approach to psychotherapy. Frankl was a Jewish physician who was sent by the Nazis to a death camp. All of his family died in the gas chambers, but he was spared because he could keep the inmates alive while the Nazis worked them to death.

In observing how humanity behaved in these desperate circumstances, Frankl discovered the essence of human freedom. The only freedom we have is the freedom to choose our response to what is happening to us. We cannot determine what happens, but we can choose what happens to what happens.

There is a dramatic story about an incident that happened to Frankl in the death camp. One day a camp guard who was exceptionally cruel noticed that Frankl still had his wedding band. The guard made Frankl extend his hand. Then, smiling gleefully, he took it off Frankl's finger.

The ring was the last possession connecting Frankl with his past. His beloved wife and children and parents had all been gassed. All of his papers and photographs had been confiscated. The guard had removed the last vestige of his identity.

As he stood looking into the mocking face of the guard, a totally unexpected thought flooded his consciousness. He realized that there was one thing, and only one thing, that the guard could not take from him: namely, *how he chose to feel* about the guard and what the guard was doing to him.

"Everything can be taken from a man but one thing," said Frankl, "the last of human freedoms to choose one's attitude in any given set of circumstances."[2]

Obviously this has been one of the themes of this book. We cannot avoid trouble and suffering. Bad things happen to good people, because bad things happen to all people. However, these things cannot *make* you bitter or angry or hopeless. You can *allow* them. But they do not determine your response. You do.

And *no one* can continue to make you feel angry, inferior, or ashamed without your permission. People can provoke these feelings in you, but you must give the feelings permission to remain. What happens to what happens to you is an inside job.

Frankl did not invent this concept of freedom, nor was he the first to discover it. This is the biblical idea reconfirmed. A living biblical example of the notion that freedom is the power to determine what happens to what happens to you is the Apostle Paul. Of all his writings, I like his letter to the church at Philippi best.

He writes the Philippians from prison when his execution is

near. He is an old, scarred warrior of the faith. He was born to wealth and privilege: a member of the elite tribe of Benjamin, educated at Tarsus by the best minds of the time, a member of the ruling order of the Jewish faith, and a zealous persecutor of the Christian sect. Now he is deserted, old, and sick in Caesar's prison in Rome, sending his farewell to the church which has remained the most faithful to the cause of Christ.

In Philippians 4:11-13, he makes an amazing statement which should speak to all who suffer. He says he's been rich and poor, with and without, comfortable and miserable. But he has learned a *great secret:* "I am content, whether I am full or hungry, whether I have too much or too little" (Philippians 4:12).

And what is this secret of contentment? He simply answers that it is the strength which Christ has given him (Philippians 4:13). He does not explain how Christ gives him this power to determine what happens to what happens to him. The power comes out of his union with Christ.

For years I wished Paul had elaborated. Then one day it occurred to me that Paul's entire life journey *was* his explanation. The Philippians didn't need a recounting of what Paul meant. He had told them his story many times. So when he said, "I have learned the secret of freedom," they knew what he meant.

When I reread through Paul's life story, I began to see that his trek to freedom had four steps. It was a process, not an instantaneous occurrence.

CONFRONTATION

The first step to freedom is being confronted with who we are, where we're going, and what our lives mean. For Paul, it culminated in the life-changing experience with God on the Damascus Road.

He was in hot pursuit of the followers of the latest Jewish

claimant to messiahship, Jesus of Nazareth. Seemingly out of the blue, he was "intersected" by the risen Lord. "Why, Paul, are you so consumed with doing violence to Me and Mine?"

In years to come, whenever Paul was challenged to legitimize his faith, whether by Jewish or Roman or Greek inquisitors—he always harkened back to this encounter. He did not find God through intellectual and emotional searching. God found him, and confronted him.

This confrontation was the culmination of a process. Paul had seen how the Christians stood up to his persecutions. He had seen how Stephen died and had heard his testimony.

Paul's education had been cosmopolitan. He saw beyond the narrow confines of Jewish culture. He had been confronting himself long before God confronted him on the road to Damascus.

You cannot begin to choose your response to suffering until you confront yourself and allow yourself to be confronted by God. You must begin to ask why you're here.

Why are you here? What are you going to do with the hand you've been dealt to play? So you've been beaten up by life; things haven't gone as you planned. What are you going to do with it?

Or maybe things haven't been all that bad for you: no great tragedies; everyone's healthy at your house. So what are you going to do with the rest of your not-too-bad life? Sail along?

> **"The Apostle Paul did not find God through intellectual and emotional searching. God found him, and confronted him."**

Or maybe things have just been super for you: no pain you can't manage, blessings galore, right place at the right time. What are you going to do with your super life? Are you going to move from success to significance?

Must you do *anything* with your life? That's probably a better question. I don't know. I do know that I must do something, besides simply exist, with mine.

All I ask you to do is ask yourself these questions—*to confront yourself.* We are the only creatures who can step outside ourselves and look at who we are.

There is a story, perhaps fictional, about the great industrialist Andrew Carnegie. He started his career with little money and power. Through shrewd business moves, he amassed one of the huge fortunes of history.

By mid-life, he stayed pretty much to himself. He traveled in his own private railroad car, and he allowed no one near him except an old black man, who served as his valet. Carnegie would board his train in the evening, get his favorite cigar and newspaper, and order the butler to remain silent. No conversation was to take place unless Carnegie initiated it.

One evening just as Carnegie had settled in with his paper and cigar, the valet approached timidly and said, "Excuse me, Mr. Carnegie!" Carnegie looked up and said, "What! Is the train on fire?" "No, sir," said the valet. "Well, then, shut up!" Carnegie ordered.

A few minutes passed and the valet approached him again. "Don't say a word!" said Carnegie.

"But, sir, you're gonna have to get off this car!" said the valet.

By now Carnegie was furious. He spat out the cigar and scattered the paper. He thundered, "And what is wrong with this car?"

"There ain't nothin' wrong with this car, sir," replied the valet. "It just ain't tied on to nothin'."

The story goes that Carnegie broke up in laughter. Later, the incident caused him to take a good look at his life. He was wealthy, powerful, and mostly alone. In fact, he lived in a gilded cage. He never knew if someone liked him or just wanted his money. Having acquired so much through subterfuge himself, he suspected everyone else of the same intentions.

He realized that he was much like his private train car. "He wasn't tied on to nothin'."

As you know, Carnegie spent the remainder of his life giving away most of what he had acquired, and millions of people have benefited.

I do not believe that anyone can live a meaningful life, whether you find yourself in hard, medium, or soft circumstances, without confrontation—without confronting yourself and allowing God to confront you. The first step to freedom is to hold your life up for scrutiny to God and to yourself.

The principle of confrontation is the key to the lasting popularity of Charles Dickens's *A Christmas Carol.* Tiny Tim and Christmas bells are the trimmings. The pull of the story is Scrooge's transformation—his being set free from his narrow little world of grasping fear. And the key to his transformation is confrontation. When he confronts the fact that he is going to die and no one will even notice, let alone care, he becomes free to respond, and generosity replaces selfishness.

CONTEMPLATION

Paul's second step to freedom was contemplation. He spent time with a mature believer in Damascus and tried to sort out what had occurred. Then he went into seclusion for three years to learn how to live from the "inside out."

Most of us live from the "outside in"; we live reactively. We wait for fortune, good or bad, to happen before we search for the inward strength to respond. We get up each day, wash, eat, and wait for life to hit us from the outside. What happens on the outside determines what happens to our "insides."

Although we can never fully prepare ourselves for the whims of fortune, we can live another way. There is a way to prepare for trouble before it occurs.

> **"Most of us live from the 'outside in'; we live reactively. We wait for fortune, good or bad, to happen before we search for the inward strength to respond."**

Look at it this way. Tragedy, trouble, and suffering always force us to look within. If there were no trouble, we would rarely look within ourselves. Suffering has produced many of the world's greatest human triumphs and caused people to create philosophy and technology. The best and finest of human culture has risen from the ashes of pain.

My point here is that we can look within ourselves *before* the trouble comes. That's what I mean by *contemplation.*

The inward life—prayer, meditation, devotion, study—is too often thought of as an end in itself. We are told to pray and read our Bibles if we want to be "good Christians" or—God help us!—"better" Christians. Whoever tells us that seems to forget what Jesus said to the rich young ruler who called Him "good." He said, "Don't call me good!"

The inward life is not a goal; it is a *means.* The purpose of contemplation is not to see who can stare at their navel the longest, but to ready us for the storms which inevitably come to our lives.

For years I had been suspicious of those holy men who retired to the desert when the world was in shambles. As I saw it, they made their reputations for piety while the world went to hell. Then I read Thomas à Kempis, Thomas Merton, Bernard of Clairvaux, and Henri Nouwen.

I had been preaching for over twenty years and had little inward life at all. I was not ashamed of it nor did I hide it. I thought most of the contemplative life could be attributed to sexual repression and a fear of getting involved in the rough-and-tumble world. I believe some of it still is, but the saints I just mentioned have opened my life to a new way of being.

First, I realized that all of these men retreated from the world in order to steel themselves to reenter it and not be absorbed by it. Until they learned to live from the inside out, they could not transform their troubles. Contemplation was a means, not an end.

I began to rework and rethink my inward life. I found out quickly that I did not enjoy my own company. I always had to be doing something or to be with someone.

The reason most suicides occur on holidays and weekends is because people literally do not know what to do with themselves when the structured routine of their lives doesn't tell them what to do. They are not friends with themselves.

Neither was I. How do you make friends with yourself? Well, this will sound silly, but I put myself in places where I had to have my own company or none at all! I went to wilderness areas to hunt and fish where no one could reach me for days.

Then I started isolating myself for short periods every day. I unplugged the phone and turned off the lights. When we built a new house, I had a soundproof bunker/study installed.

Prayer and silence have now become major parts of my daily routine. I cannot explain what I am about to tell you. I can only state that it is true. Life's troubles do not seem to paralyze me as they did before I began to "exercise my inside muscles."

The eighteen months preceding this writing project should have been as stressful as any I have ever faced. I have had four surgeries. I have searched three months for a lost three-year-old granddaughter, found her, brought her to live with us in all of her agony, dealt with her parents, bonded with her, and lost her. I have teetered on the edge of financial bankruptcy, lost all of our savings, and gone through a building program at the church. Several of my soul mates who helped start our church pulled out and started a new church down the street in the opposite direction from the group I mentioned earlier. Their pastor is yet another former minister friend whom I gave a job after he had lost his family and church several years ago.

Well, don't weep for me! I am bruised, battered, and broken. But I am not defeated. I'm like an old jalopy. The body's all bent up but the engine, the inside life, is still humming.

Harry Emerson Fosdick used to compare life's journey to the way ancient mariners sailed their ships.[3] Some followed the coastline and never left the sight of land. Of course, they never went very far either. That's called *conservatism.*

Some just launched out hoping to find their destination by sheer luck. Of course, they either perished or didn't know where they were when they got there. That's called *rebellion.*

Others simply followed behind other vessels who were supposed to know the way. Most of the time they reached their destination. That's called *conformity.*

But some ancient mariners developed an on-board compass, said Fosdick. They didn't have to hug the coast, launch out foolishly, or follow others. They are called *pioneers.*

Contemplation is developing your own on-board compass, tending to the inward dimension of your life. Make friends with yourself and God on the inside. If you can do this *before* the storm, you can determine what happens to what happens to you.

PARTICIPATION

Paul moved beyond contemplation to *participation.* He came back from his retreat and got into the thick of things. Although the Christian movement was nearly a decade old, no one had realized that Christ was for the whole world. Christianity was little more than a new Jewish sect in the eyes of Jesus' own disciples.

Paul picked up the banner of worldwide missions to the Gentiles. He refused to sit around complaining about what life was doing to him. He was never again driven by his demons. He was now drawn by his dreams.

Hear that phrase again: *Not driven by demons but drawn by dreams.* Paul dived into life and withstood a constant barrage of troubles because he was drawn by his dream. In the midst of trouble, he always resorted to participation instead of paralysis.

People who are *driven* move out into life from a position of emptiness. They have to "go and get" in order to fill up the void within. When they fail, they're defeated. But people who are drawn by their dreams move out into life from a position of fullness. Their ambition is to pour out what they have. Instead of "go and get," they "go and give." In other words, driven people have an empty tank, and they spend their lives trying to fill it. Drawn people have a full tank, and they spend their lives trying to empty it.

You can see what a difference this makes when tragedy strikes. If I am drawn by a dream, then obstacles become challenges. If I am driven, then obstacles become barriers I cannot climb over.

"I have learned how to be full in all circumstances," said an aged Paul. But one chapter earlier he says, "I do not claim that I have already succeeded or have already become perfect... the one thing I do, however, is to forget what is behind and do my best to reach what is ahead... in order to win the prize which is God's call through Christ Jesus to the life above" (Philippians 3:12-14).

I am not advocating the technique of staying busy as a cure for handling trouble. In some cases, it's the only thing that keeps us sane, but participation is not "staying busy." Participation is being drawn by a calling which makes our pain, however severe, seem momentary.

I know an extraordinary woman who exemplifies being drawn by a dream. Her story took place in a culture and circumstances so foreign to ours that you may get distracted by your cultural biases when you hear it.

She was born in a rural Muslim country, the daughter of a peasant. Women had no status socially or politically in her culture. But as a child she taught herself to read from books given to her by merchants who purchased wool at her village.

When she reached the age of twelve, she convinced her father to "sell" her into a Turkish family who lived in the capital city of her country. She would be a household servant. Her father could keep all of the money. All she wanted was room and board and the privilege of attending school.

At sixteen, she had won the affections of her "employers." She had also read the Bible and learned of the world beyond her. She developed a relationship with God and became a devout Christian on her own. She also led the school in academic honors.

She began to pray for a way to escape her circumstances. If she went back home, her father would sell her to a goat herder. She would bring a good price, for she was and is very beautiful. There seemed no way out, but she kept praying and focusing on her dream.

One of her employers' friends, who frequently visited the home, was many years her senior, a widower, a Turkish citizen, and a man of some means. One day she felt led to speak to him of her dream of going to the free world. She also ventured to tell him that she was a Christian, and she believed God would somehow answer her prayers.

The older gentleman confessed that he, too, was a Christian but kept it a secret because most of his business dealings were with Muslims. "Every time I go to the mosque for prayers, I actually pray in Jesus' name," he said. "They would take my head if they knew, but I think Allah and Jesus laugh plenty."

**"If I am drawn by a dream, then obstacles
become challenges. I am driven,
then obstacles become barriers
I cannot climb over."**

They both agreed to pray for God to show them how the girl could escape her circumstances. One day some months later when she came home from school, her father was there. Her keepers informed her that their Turkish friend had asked for her hand in marriage and that her father had consented, for a tidy sum, of course.

Then the Turkish gentleman walked in. When they were alone, he told her that God had shown him a plan. She could go to America and continue her education. Whether she became his wife "in fact" was her decision completely. When she finished college, she could decide whether to return to Turkey as his wife or remain in America.

She came to America speaking only the English she had taught herself from books. After graduating with honors from a large university, she divorced the Turkish gentleman. Later she married an American. They have children and a wonderful home. She owns a thriving business. And God is no stranger to them.

I do not know to this day if she consummated her marriage to the older man, and I don't care. I do love to hear her speak of how dreams can draw us through the thickets of impossibility. I do love to watch her put her faith to work. What most people see as stumbling blocks are but stepping-stones to her. As the saying goes, while others break, she breaks records.

ANTICIPATION

The final stage of Paul's victory over his suffering was what I call *anticipation*. Instead of bitterness, which we would expect from one who had sacrificed and ended up on death row, all we hear from him is excitement about the future. He has complete confidence and peace about what is to come.

In the first part of his letter to the Philippians, he says that his imprisonment has really proved to be a blessing. For one thing, some of his jailers have come to know Christ as a result of his sharing with them. Also several Roman Christians have begun to preach out of necessity because he is in jail. Some are preaching from impure motives, he says, but Christ is being preached, and that's what counts (Philippians 1:12-20).

Then Paul talks about his dying. He says he's caught between the desire to go on and be with God in the afterlife and the desire to continue his mission on earth. To live here is to be with Christ, but to die is even better (Philippians 1:20-21).

The final step to the power of determining what happens to what happens to us is the absence of the fear of death. Freedom ultimately means freedom from the fear of death, but we cannot be free from this fear unless we see the future as friendly.

Frankl says this was confirmed many times by those death-camp inmates who survived while others died. " 'The prisoner who lost faith in the future, his future, was doomed. With his loss of belief in the future, he also lost his spiritual hold. He let himself decline and become subject to mental and physical decay."[4]

At the beginning of this book, I told of having to take our daughter to Massachusetts and leave her in an expensive school. I said we had managed the tuition even though it was the equivalent of my salary. I want to tell you now how we managed.

First, I went to the church leaders and asked for a raise. My annual salary was twelve thousand dollars plus housing, which was the most the church had ever paid anyone. However, they did contribute about fifty thousand dollars per year to mission causes beyond our town and subsidized a local mission at about twenty thousand dollars annually.

I figured our handicapped child's need for schooling might qualify as a "mission." They did, too, to the tune of fifty dollars per month.

We sold both cars to pay for the first semester and bought an old jalopy.

One day I received a call from Henry Sears, president and majority owner of one of the two banks in town. "Could I come see him?" he asked.

Henry was known both for his honesty and his hard-nosed approach to banking. When I walked in, he greeted me in his no-nonsense manner and said, "I like what you're doing for our town. I also like your common sense sermons."

"But you've never heard me speak," I said.

"I never miss hearing you," he said. "I listen on the radio every Sunday morning. I also know about your Sunday evening program of having ministers and congregations from other denominations as guests for dialogue. Heck, the Catholics and the Baptists are speaking to each other for the first time in our town's history! I understand that you and the Church of Christ preacher were seen playing golf together. I hope you both keep your jobs."

He took a breath and said, "Well, enough of the niceties. I hear you have a handicapped child. I'm going to put you in the cattle-feeding business. We'll buy two hundred head and feed them for one hundred fifty days and sell them. I'll lend you the money."

"But what if we lose?" I protested.

"Well, we will just roll the loss into the next two hundred

head," he said. "And we'll keep running up the tab till you make some money. You got any collateral?"

He saw the look on my face and said, "I didn't think so. Let me ask you, can you keep a secret? I mean from everyone, even your wife?"

"No, sir," I said. "I can keep it from everyone except my wife. We don't keep secrets."

"Okay," he nodded. "I am personally going to sign all of your notes. If this information comes back to me, I'll call 'em all due and payable!"

Cindy went to school. I endorsed my paycheck back to the church, including the six hundred dollars per year raise, for the next two years.

Then Henry contracted amyotrophic lateral sclerosis, Lou Gehrig's disease. As you know, it's an insidious killer. The muscles slowly degenerate until only the eyelids and the heart function. Yet the patient never loses his complete mental faculties. He is literally imprisoned within a motionless body.

Henry made it clear that he wanted no artificial life-support systems. As his condition deteriorated, we became close friends. He would chase all of the nurses and family out of the room, and we would talk. He wanted to hear my jokes more than anything else.

Then there was a ray of hope from the medical community. An experimental drug was being tested with some promise in Houston. Henry decided to give it a try. But before the drug could be fully administered, he developed pneumonia. His dilemma was either to die from the pneumonia or to go on a respirator and give the drug a chance to work.

He chose the respirator, but the drug didn't work. Now, no one would unplug the machine. The very thing he didn't want to happen had happened.

When he came home to our small town hospital, I went to see him. When we were alone, he managed to whisper that he wanted to talk about death and the afterlife. "Can you give me a word of hope?" he mumbled. "I need something to keep with me before I can no longer talk or read. Help me, preacher. Don't give me any B.S. Give me a word of hope."

My mind raced. I was praying at warp speed. All that came to mind was a verse from Psalm 42. I gave him what I had been given. The psalmist complains to God, "Why have you forgotten me? Why must I go on suffering?" But that's in verses 9 and 10.

Verse 11, the one I remembered, is God's response: "Why art thou so downcast? Why art thou so troubled? Hope thou in God! And thou shalt stand someday again to praise Him!" (MSICIV).

In the months that followed, I visited Henry often. I would tell him the jokes he loved. We would pray. When he could still whisper, he would say, "Psalm 42—Hope thou in God!" Later, when he could move only his fingers, he would waggle four and then two.

The last day I saw him, he could only blink his eyes. I told him his favorite joke and prayed silently as I held his hand. When I looked into his eyes, they blinked four times, then two times, and teared.

The future had become Henry's friend. He couldn't control what happened to him, but he could control what happened to what happened to him. "Hope thou in God! And thou shalt stand again to praise His name!"

14

There's a "Yes" in Every Mess

I love Robert Schuller's "tough times never last but tough people do." That's right! But what makes people tough?

I have maintained throughout this book that the power to metabolize suffering comes from principles which are chiseled into the bedrock of the soul by the grace of God. I have given each of these principles a catchy title, not in order to be cute, but to help you remember them as you tackle the bad times.

Three themes are woven throughout these principles: Faith, hope, and love. *Faith = trust + risk.* That means trusting God enough to risk getting on with life in the midst of pain. *Hope = trust + risk + joy*—not just getting on with it, but also getting on with it in laughter and celebration of what is to come. *Love = trust + risk + joy + caring*—pouring out ourselves for those who are as wounded as we, which means everyone.

These are the only things that last, the only permanents in the universe. "These three things remain" (1 Corinthians 13:13). To believe this is to garner the power to make the bad times over *for good.* Faithing, hoping, and loving are not *what* it's all about: they are *all* it's all about! If I were required to reduce all the principles which I have used for faithing, hoping, and loving into one sentence, I would say, *"There's a yes in every mess."* Hardly a day passes that I don't use it.

But when I say, "there's a yes in every mess," I am not advocating the look-for-a-silver-lining optimism which we often hear in motivational speeches. Oh, I believe we should indeed look for the silver lining, but in reality every dark cloud doesn't have one.

Optimism is a wonderful trait. I would choose it over pessimism any day. But things are not going to get better simply because we will them. In fact, as I have said often enough in this book, things are more likely to get worse. I saw a cartoon that pictured Jesus on the cross. He's speaking to the onlookers and says, "If I'm OK and you're OK and it's OK, what am I doing *here?"*

The philosophy of *inevitable progress* which has ruled the Western world for two centuries has always seemed curious to me. Who says that progress is inevitable? And what is progress anyway?

I look at the present disintegration of socialistic communism, and I cannot help but wonder if Eastern Europeans are not more hungry for the material prosperity of the West than they are for democratic government. Democracy is hard work, as they are learning, and most Americans don't even bother to vote. What a pity if the entire world embraces consumerism in the name of freedom!

The yes I see in every mess that exists in our world is not based upon any political, material, or social system.

"There's a yes in every mess" came to me one day when I was reading 2 Corinthians 1 in the Good News Bible translation of the New Testament. In verses 19-20, it says, "Jesus Christ, the Son of God ... is not one who is 'Yes' and 'No.' On the contrary, he is God's 'Yes' ... the 'Yes' to all of God's promises." I checked out the translation in the Greek New Testament, and it is accurate.

Jesus Christ, the Son of God, is the yes I see in the mess of human existence. My hopes for the planet do not rest on the natural evolution of the human race but on the supernatural evolution of the human race—on God raising us to a new level.

I believe God is in all things working, the literal translation of Romans 8:28. Not, "All things work together for good for those who love God" but "God is in all things, working His good."

The yes in every mess is "God with us," Jesus Christ. If God did not become a human, one who dirtied his diaper and was tempted by the opposite sex and faced everything we face, there is no yes in our mess.

If just once there wasn't a human who obeyed the Father all the way, there is no yes. If God didn't raise Him up, there's no yes.

We make extraordinary claims about Him. Either they are true or they are not. If they are not, then no is written across the face of this world.

> **"Jesus Christ, the Son of God, is the yes I see in the mess of human existence."**

But I have met Him, you see. I know that my experience can be thoroughly explained by a psychiatrist and explained away by a nihilist. No matter. He lives. And because He lives, there's a yes in every mess.

THE YES IN THE GLOBAL MESS

Recently I have begun to do some thinking about the future of our world. The holocaust peddlers are having a field day with their charts and apocalyptic scriptures.

There are indeed so many barriers separating people from each other on this little spaceship earth, and religion seems to be among the leaders in keeping people apart. Do away with religious differences and a grand portion of the world's enmities would vanish.

I believe that technology has already begun to shrink the world economically and politically. The globalization of all of life is now a reality.

The world is becoming one in every area except the spiritual. When you look at how far we have to go in unifying mankind in spirit, you find a real mess. I have been seeking an answer as to how Jesus can be the yes in this global mess, and I believe that the problem lies mostly with those of us who call ourselves Christians.

Jesus' original disciples were called "followers of the Way," not "Christians," which means *little replicas of Christ.* As we have already said, Jesus did not come to start a new religion. He came to teach us how to relate to God, neighbor, and self. Religion is what we have done to Christ's Way.

When He said to His disciples, "I am the Way, the Truth, and the Life; no one goes to the Father except by me" (John 14:6), I don't believe He was summarily condemning all non-Christians to hell. Rather, He was calling all of humanity to His way of doing life.

No one had ever called God a Father. Up to that time, God had been thought of as a power, a force, and a terror, but not as a loving father. Maybe He was saying simply that the only way to know God as He knew Him, as a loving Father, was by doing life the way He did it.

I cannot carry this thought further, because it has only recently begun to sink into my soul. But I do mean that I believe Jesus' way of treating people, self, and God is the yes which can cure the spiritual mess which threatens to kill us all.

A good beginning might be to realize that His view of non-retaliation is not mere idealism. We should know by now that using violence to cure violence kills people but breeds more violence.

For example, think of the tremendous advance in world peace if Arabs and Israelis were to decide to abandon the eye-for-an-eye mentality which has ruled their consciousness since Esau and Jacob.

You think this is pie-eyed? Well, it has already worked once! Anwar Sadat, a Muslim and president of Egypt, used Jesus' tactic to trigger peace with Israel. He declared that the vicious cycle of violence would not be continued from his side. Israel reciprocated. The peace exists to this day.

At some point someone always has to leave the last insult unanswered. That was Jesus' teaching, not pie-eyed idealism. And it is the hard reality of peace.

We must find a means of applying Jesus' way to all of the global messes which threaten us. I am not qualified even to suggest what this means, except to say that Christians must begin to think "trans-Christian," that is, beyond our own narrow interpretations of Jesus' teachings.

Frankly, I think we have made only a meager beginning in trying to apply what He taught on a global scale. Our missionary efforts have mostly been designed to win people rather than to love them into existence. There has been more Americanization than Christianization.

THE YES IN THE PERSONAL MESS

I have tried to say that there's a yes in every failure. If you have blown it, you can find Christ in the ash heap. That's where He stays most often. He's the yes in the mess of your failures.

I love the story of Thomas Edison's attempt to invent the electric light. His faithful assistant, who had been with him throughout his many discoveries, grew despondent. "We've tried 714 experiments," he said. "We have failed. We have made no progress."

"We have made great progress!" countered Edison. "We know 714 things that won't work!"

Make a list of your failures. Then write at the top of the page: "Things I no longer have to try."

> *"Make a list of your failures.*
> *Then write at the top of the page:*
> *'Things I no longer have to try.'"*

I have tried to say there's a yes in every mistake. I made a great mistake in coming to Austin, Texas, twenty years ago. I came to a church for which I could not have been more ill-suited. I knew it within days after my arrival.

For seven years, I gutted it out. Mostly it was pride. But Christ was in the midst of the mistake. Two of the greatest "years" of my life resulted. My son was born in a city with medical facilities that saved his life. Had I not moved there, he would have died at birth. Like Abraham, I got to bring my boy down from the mountain.

The second great yes was Riverbend Church. From the moment I laid eyes on the land, which was offered as a gift by two young business adventurers, I knew why I had labored under the yoke for seven years. God wanted me to build a great church.

I have tried to say that there is a yes even in our sins. The place where the broken bone heals is stronger than it was before it was broken.

And I have tried to say that there's a yes in every tragedy, even the worst and foulest.

Carlyle Marney told me that he was summoned to the home of a family in his church one summer afternoon in the days before air conditioning. A young mother had placed her two-year-old son near the upstairs window so he could catch the breeze during his nap. He crawled over the window sill, tumbled down the roof, and was impaled upon the picket fence below.

For a long time, Marney held the mother and cried with her. Finally she said, "Marney, where was God when my baby was dying on that stake?" Marney sobbed, took a deep breath, and said, "I do not know. I suppose He was in the same place as when His Son died the same way."

One of the "yesses" in our messes is the commonality that happens among all of us who hurt. Suffering is perhaps the greatest eraser of the lines that separate us. The fellowship of the wounded is a yes in the mess of human existence.

I won't forget awakening from the anesthetic in the ICU to hear a fellow pastor, with whom I had had many battles, praying the sweetest prayer I ever heard for my recovery. He had been where I was. Our theological differences seemed ridiculous after that.

I won't forget the night little Cindy came into my study. We were to leave for Massachusetts in two days. She was barely eight years old.

"Do I have to go?" she pleaded.

"Yes, little one. You must."

"Because I'm deaf. Right?"

"Yes. You know you must go."

"Daddy, will you ask God to let me hear like you and Mommy hear? Then I won't have to go."

"I have asked many times. I have asked Him every day of your life."

"But would you ask Him now?" How could I do otherwise? I knelt and prayed. My heart was like a great stone in my chest. When I finished, she said, "What did God say, Daddy?"

I had to admit that He hadn't said anything. There was nothing but an overwhelming silence. I looked into her expectant bright eyes and began to sob in great heaves.

Then I felt her tiny hand patting me on my shoulder. "Don't cry, Daddy. Jesus will take care of me."

A child's courage and faith shined the light into the darkest dungeon of my sorrow. "The light shines in the darkness and the darkness cannot extinguish it."

I won't forget the day I came home from the long trip to leave Cindy in Massachusetts. My tear ducts were all used up, I thought. Into the driveway came Homer Hanna's old Pontiac. He walked in and said, "I just came over to cry with you." We did, and he went home.

An elderly pastor was asked to describe how he viewed the ministry. He said when he was young he saw his people as if they were in this polluted mucky river, drowning. His job was to stand on the high bank and shout instructions on how to get out of the muck.

In mid-life, he said, he saw himself as creeping down to the water's edge, leaning over, and pulling people out.

But after about thirty years, he decided his job was to jump into the muck with them, hold on to them, and tread like crazy.

I decided to write this book as a fellow "treader in the muck," for that's where I have found Jesus most often. Jesus is the name of the yes in every mess. He is the name of our species, too. He's what we are all coming to.

When you know that, your bad times can be over for good.

Notes

Introduction

1. cf. Kenneth Erickson, *The Power of Praise* (St. Louis, Missouri: Concordia Publishing, 1984), 91-92.
2. Lee Atwater, with Todd Brewster, "The Last Campaign," *Life* magazine, XIV (February 1991): 58-62.
3. Ibid., 62.
4. Kennon Callahan, lecture, May 1991.

Chapter 1: Grace Is the Grit

1. Karl Menninger, with Martin Mayman and Paul Pruysek, *The Vital Balance* (New York: Viking Press, 1963), 204-205.
2. Ibid., 205.
3. cf. David A. Redding, *Before You Call, I Will Answer* (Old Tappan, New Jersey: Fleming H. Revell, 1985), 24ff.
4. Ibid.
5. Harry Emerson Fosdick, *Living Under Tension* (New York: Harper & Row, 1941), 209.

Chapter 2: Trouble's the Trigger

1. Bruce Larson, *The Meaning and Mystery of Being Human* (Waco, Texas: Word Books, 1978), 25.
2. cf. Malcolm Muggeridge, *A Third Testament* (New York: Ballantine Books, 1976), 48.
3. Ibid., 60-61.

Chapter 4: Ruts Ain't Roots

1. For a complete discussion of the Irenaean concept and its development in the pre-Latin church, see John Hick, *Evil and The Love of God* (New York: Harper and Row, 1966), 217ff.
2. Carlyle Marney, *The Coming Faith* (Nashville: Abingdon Press, 1970), 49-50.
3. John Killinger, *For God's Sake Be Human* (Waco: Word Books, 1970), 30.
4. Stephen Brown, *When Being Good Isn't Good Enough* (Nashville: Thomas Nelson Publishing, 1990), 203ff.
5. Ibid.

Chapter 5: Miracles Happen in Miracle Territory

1. cf. Harry Emerson Fosdick, *Living Under Tension* (New York: Harper & Row, 1941), 58.
2. Denton A. Cooley, *Reflections and Observations* (Austin, Texas: Eakin Press, 1984), 77.
3. cf. Norman Vincent Peale, *The Power of the Plus Factor* (Old Tappan, New Jersey: Fleming H. Revell, 1987), 158.

Chapter 6: The Steam of Self-Esteem

1. Gary Smalley and John Trent, *The Blessing* (Nashville: Thomas Nelson, 1986).
2. Myron Madden, *The Power to Bless* (New York: Abingdon Press, 1970), 15ff.

Chapter 7: Every Mountain Is a Foothill

1. See Henri J. M. Nouwen, *The Wounded Healer* (Garden City, New York: Doubleday, 1972), 83-84.
2. See Keith Miller, *The Becomers* (Waco, Texas: Word Books, 1973), 159ff.

3. cf. Roland Bainton, *Here I Stand* (New York: Abingdon Press, 1950), 304.
4. *Austin American Statesman*, 24 May 1991, sec. D3.
5. See J. W. Kentch, *The American Drama Since 1918* (New York: Harper & Row, 1939)

Chapter 8: Winning Is Beginning

1. See John Claypool, *Tracks of a Fellow Struggler* (Waco, Texas: Word Books, 1974), 45-62.
2. Ibid.
3. Erickson, *The Power of Praise,* 11.
4. Blaise Pascal, translated by W. F. Trotter, *Pensées* (New York: E. P. Dutton, 1958), 85, Number 245.
5. cf. Thomas Fry, *They Dared to Dream* (Waco, Texas: Word Books, 1972), 61.

Chapter 9: The Little Path Is the Middle Path

1. Gerald Mann, *Why Does Jesus Make Me Nervous?* (Waco, Texas: Word Books, 1980).
2. cf. *Austin American Statesman,* 1 June 1991, D1.

Chapter 10: There's Clout in Doubt

1. cf. Viktor Frankl, *Man's Search for Meaning* (New York: Washington Square Press, 1963), xiii.
2. Harry Emerson Fosdick, *Dear Mr. Brown* (New York: Harper & Row, 1961), 69.
3. cf. Lyle W. Dorsett, *And God Came In* (New York: Jove Books, 1974), 53.
4. Corrie Ten Boom, *Tramp for the Lord* (New York: Jove Books, 1974), 53.
5. See C. S. Lewis, *God in the Dock* (Grand Rapids, Michigan: William B. Eerdman's, 1970), 287-300.

Chapter 11: It's Grateful or Hateful

1. R. Lofton Hudson, *Grace Is Not a Blue-Eyed Blond* (Waco, Texas: Word Books, 1968), 25-36.
2. Claypool, *Tracks,* 63-84.
3. *Austin American Statesman,* 20 November 1989.

Chapter 12: Choose to Lose

1. See Nikus Kazantzakis, *Report to Grecko.*
2. C. S. Lewis, *The Screwtape Letters* (New York: The Macmillan Co., 1961), 3.
3. Dorothy Sayers, *Christian Letters to a Post-Christian World* (Grand Rapids: Wm. B. Eerdman's, 1969), xi.
4. Carlyle Marney, *Priests to Each Other* (Valley Forge: Judson Press, 1974), 67-84.
5. M. Scott Peck, *The Different Drum* (New York: Simon and Schuster, 1983, 297.

Chapter 13: It's What Happens to What Happens to You

1. William Ernest Henley, "Invictus" in *The Best Loved Poems of the American People* (Garden City, New York: Garden City Books, 1936).
2. Frankl, *Man's Search,* 104.
3. Fosdick, *Living Under Tension,* 182ff.
4. Frankl, *Man's Search,* 117.

About the Author

GERALD MANN is a minister, writer, businessman, TV and radio personality, humorist, legislative chaplain, public speaker, and a voice for common sense Christianity. He has a diversified background and experience in human relations which have enriched his views on life and have made him a very able and sensitive counselor.

Dr. Mann has been featured in *TV Guide, USA Today, Advertising Age* and *Texas Monthly.* He has been quoted by "NBC Nightly News,' Paul Harvey, and nearly every major newspaper in America, including *US News and World Report* and *The Wall Street Journal.* Currently, he is the host of a live, call-in, national TV program which is seen four times weekly on VISN Network.

Author of several books, Mann is a communicator whose universal messages apply to everyday life. He is the senior pastor of Riverbend Baptist Church in Austin, Texas—a church of over three thousand members. He lives with his wife, Lois, in Austin, and has three children: Cindy, Stacey, and J.J.